Performing the Psalms

DAVE BLAND & DAVID FLEER, EDS.

WITH ESSAYS AND SERMONS BY
Walter Brueggemann,
J. Clinton McCann Jr.,
Paul Scott Wilson,
and Others

CHALICE
P R E S S
ST. LOUIS, MISSOURI

Cover and interior design: Elizabeth Wright

This book is printed on acid-free, recycled paper.

Visit Chalice Press on the World Wide Web at
www.chalicepress.com

10 9 8 7 6 5 4 3 2 1   05 06 07 08 09

Library of Congress Cataloging-in-Publication Data

Performing the psalms: with essays and sermons by Walter Brueggemann, J. Clinton McCann Jr., Paul Scott Wilson, and others / [edited by] David Fleer and Dave Bland.
    p. cm.
 ISBN 13: 978-0-827229-83-6 (pbk. : alk. paper)
 ISBN 10: 0-827229-83-6
 1. Bible. O.T. Psalms–Criticism, interpretation, etc. I. Fleer, David. II. Bland, Dave.
 BS1430.52P47 2005
 223'.206–dc22
          Printed in the United States of America

                                                    2004030145

To Mae, Josh, Luke, and Nate
with gratitude for their sustaining love.

DAVID FLEER

To Nancy, Nathan, Jennifer, Justin, and B.J.,
who enrich the meaning of life, love, and friendship.

DAVE BLAND

Contents

Acknowledgments

Special thanks to Josh Fleer for careful reading of several manuscripts in their early stages, Trent Butler for his strong encouragement, Sarah Tasic for her thoughtful editorial guidance, and to the preachers from across denominational lines and geographical divide who are the Reforming Center of Protestant Christianity and provide the grist and energy for the Sermon Seminar where this volume had its origins.

Contributors

DAVE BLAND–For more than two decades, Dave Bland has devoted his life to preaching tenures with the Eastside Church of Christ in Portland, Oregon, and, currently, with the White Station congregation in Memphis. Dave complements his life's activity in preaching with a background in rhetoric (Ph.D., University of Washington) and has long cultivated an interest in wisdom literature. In addition to preaching, Dave serves as full-time professor of homiletics at Harding University Graduate School of Religion in Memphis.

WALTER BRUEGGEMANN–Walter Brueggemann is past president of the Society of Biblical Literature, William Marcellus McPheeters Professor of Old Testament, emeritus at Columbia Seminary, and minister in the United Church of Christ. Well-known for more than four decades as a biblical interpreter who demonstrates how ancient texts speak to human life, Walt has taught and published widely in the prophetic materials of the Old Testament and on the Psalms.

JEFF M. CHRISTIAN–Jeff Christian has spent the last thirteen years ministering to churches in Texas through the pulpit as well as sharing life together with those communities of faith. He has been preaching with the Glenwood Church of Christ in Tyler, Texas, since 2002. He received his M.Div. from Abilene Christian University, where he is now in their Doctor of Ministry program. He loves the church, the ministry of preaching, the power of the spoken word, and the unique ways that the voice of culture blends with the voice of the gospel. He devotes himself to study in homiletics, philosophy, rhetoric, scripture, and culture in order to help the communities of faith that he serves to fully engage the world imagined by scripture.

RONALD COX–Honored in 2003 as "Most Influential Faculty Member" by the students of Rochester College in Rochester

Hills, Michigan, Ron Cox has found his professional niche in bringing together students and scripture. Ron has sustained his efforts in the classroom through personal research on the Psalms and their interpretation. In addition to the essay in this volume, Ron has written on patristic exegesis of Psalm 45 (to appear in a forthcoming collection) and is currently studying the pop-cultural influence of the psalms (especially in the songs of U2). Ron recently completed his University of Notre Dame dissertation on New Testament christology.

DAVID FLEER–David Fleer's devotion to preaching first found expression through a long-tenured pulpit ministry with the Vancouver Church of Christ in the state of Washington. His Ph.D. in Speech Communication at the University of Washington moved him into teaching at Rochester College, where he is currently professor of religion and communication and vice president of church relations. David's work is characterized as a thoughtful and passionate attempt to walk afresh in the world of scripture, that readers and listeners may experience the reality of the gospel of God.

JOHN MARK HICKS–John Mark Hicks serves as professor of theology at David Lipscomb University in Nashville, Tennessee, and also on the ministry staff at the Woodmont Hills Church of Christ. He has authored several books including *Yet Will I Trust Him: Understanding God in a Suffering World* (1999) and a commentary on 1 & 2 Chronicles (2001). He has a special interest in the lament material of the Old Testament.

JAMES HOWELL–After earning a Ph.D. from Duke, focusing on the Psalter and studying with Fr. Roland Murphy, James Howell has spent the past twenty-three years in parish ministry, serving four congregations: rural, inner-city, suburban, and urban. Now he is the senior pastor of the 4,500-member Myers Park United Methodist Church in Charlotte, North Carolina. The author of eight books and numerous articles, he has been an advocate for the teaching ministry of the clergy and has also been deeply engaged in social justice issues and ministry with the poor in his local communities and in Eastern Europe, Africa, Asia, and Latin America.

MARK LOVE–Mark Love is assistant professor of ministry and director of ministry events at Abilene Christian University, Abilene, Texas. Before assuming his current responsibilities, Mark served in congregational ministry for seventeen years, the last eleven as Minister of the Word for the East County Church of Christ in Gresham, Oregon. Mark teaches both evangelism and preaching courses at ACU. Mark is passionate about the ways that the gospel creates worlds of meaningful discourse.

J. CLINTON MCCANN JR.–Clinton McCann was a preacher and pastor for ten years in North Carolina, during which time he also received a Ph.D. in Biblical Studies from Duke University. Since 1987, he has taught Biblical Studies at Eden Theological Seminary in Webster Groves, Missouri, where he is now the Evangelical Professor of Biblical Interpretation. Clint served from 1989 to 1998 as chair of the Psalms program unit for the Society of Biblical Literature; and he is the author of several books and essays on the Psalms, including the Psalms commentary in *The New Interpreter's Bible* and *Preaching the Psalms* (coauthored with James Howell).

PAUL SCOTT WILSON–Paul Wilson is Professor of Homiletics at Emmanuel College of Victoria University in the University of Toronto, where he has taught since 1981. He has published numerous books on preaching and is past president of the Academy of Homiletics. He is honorary minister at St. Stephen's-on-the-Hill United Church in Mississauga, Ontario, and has served churches in northern Ontario and Toronto. His M.Div. is from Emmanuel College, and his Ph.D. is from King's College, University of London.

INTRODUCTION

Performing the Psalms and the World Imagined in the Psalter

DAVE BLAND AND DAVID FLEER

This volume originated in the Rochester College Sermon Seminar during May, 2004, when nearly two hundred ministers from thirty-four states, three countries and more than fifteen denominations gathered for the common purpose of preparing to preach from the Psalms. While a majority of preachers came from the Churches of Christ, one identifying mark united us all. This ecumenical mix of Free and United Methodists, American and Southern Baptists, Churches of Christ, and others was joined as the Reforming Center of Protestant Christianity.

Church historians have long noted Protestant Christianity's evolution into *two parties:* evangelical and mainline, conservative and liberal. In the last few years, however, we have experienced an original migration to a reforming *center,* where large numbers from each party are finding they share substantive Christian views. Evangelical and mainline Christians are discovering that they hold in common absolute devotion to an essential issue: Scripture envisions a transcendent being and human existence more real than the illusory world offered by the dominant ideologies of our culture.[1] This Reforming Center is a community that desires to be lifted past old barriers and labels, and longs for a new paradigm for reading and preaching from the world created in scripture.

We believe that the Bible desires to shape us by imagining a world into which it invites us to enter. We believe that these biblical narratives make one claim that positions them above all rivals for our lives: the Bible is from God. The Bible casts God's desires for reality into the hearts of those who believe its story enough to live in it. "All scripture is inspired by God" and thus seeks to capture Christians' imagination. For this reason we concur with Garrett Green's claim, "The religious vision of 'what the world is like,' embodied in the Scriptures of the Old and New Testaments, is for Christians the paradigmatic norm for human life and thought. Christian faith can be characterized accordingly as faithful imagination–living in conformity to the vision rendered by the Word of God in the Bible."[2] What then is this faithful imagination and how does it impact preaching from the Psalms?

Faithful imagination begins with our *position* toward scripture. For preachers to engage the world the Psalms imagine, we begin by not explaining the world that created the Psalms, but by understanding the world the Psalms create. Nor do we approach the text driving a moving van weighted down with political agendas expecting divine approval. Nor do we enter the text with backpacks bulging full with our personal issues, expecting God to give us a shoulder.

If, however, we check our political allegiances and release our personal demands, once in the imagined world of the Psalms we may be better able to engage the worlds the Psalms produce, deconstructing one world as we begin to envision another. We believe that to engage the deepest levels of human need we must move into the world of the Bible, where there exists a place preachers may invite their congregations to enter and learn to think and live anew. Preaching thus involves an imaginative leap where God speaks through scripture and continues to work in new ways. *This* is the essential position at the heart of the preacher's task.

How shall preachers offer a vision beyond themselves and draw congregations to life as the vision is uttered and imagined in the Psalter? How shall preachers speak from the Psalms of the reality of the transcendent God who, through these texts and their implied narratives, longs to claim central position in our lives? These concerns are at the heart of this volume and unearth a bevy of thrilling questions and possibilities: What would happen if we abandoned using the Bible to illustrate our prior theological notions and personal needs? What would happen if we learned to see the Bible as imagining a reality capable of recasting our human agendas to fit God's greater purpose? What would happen if we turned to scripture for insights beyond us, for a word that did not serve our constructions of desire and need? What would happen if we allowed the Bible to form us into a community encountered in scripture by the living Lord?[3] What would happen if we allowed ourselves to live in this new paradigm that grants the Bible a reality-defining power over the church and thus creates "an alternative story of the world?"[4] What would happen if the church became the imaginative projection of the biblical text? What if we allowed God through scripture to change us?

This volume's response to these questions is crafted in two parts. The book's first half is a collection of heuristic essays that begin a lively dialogue by orienting readers to the worlds clearly conceived in Psalms. The discussion continues with the sermons in the volume's second section. These appropriate both the essays' orientation and specific detail to provide grist and inspiration for the reader's homiletic mind.

In the first essay, Walter Brueggemann sets out a generative strategy for the preacher to draw the congregation to life as it is imagined in the Psalms. This strategy, Brueggemann anticipates, will transpose a congregation into "Psalmic dialogue" of depth and staying power by having the Psalms' narrative re-performed in its life. Using a collection of instances from the Psalter, Brueggemann shows that the very recital of counter-narratives subverts our more familiar and hopeless worlds.[5] In the narrative re-performance of the Psalms we make the generic particular, even creating new superscriptions for a thicker and

more complex sermonic performance. Just as biblical superscriptions are an act of imaginative imposition, so the new
superscriptions replicate the canonical process and move the
classic utterances of the Psalter close to the lived congregational
reality.

Brueggemann's second essay defines limit expressions as
the deep recesses of genuine humanness that give utterance to
the deep conflicted places where holiness is at work for
transformative healing and newness. Brueggemann maintains
that the Psalter is the truest collage of limit expression in human
history. The pulpit is one of the few venues left in our society
for such honest speech, "the most radical social action in which
the church can participate." Brueggemann thus calls preachers
to repent of taming and domesticating the Psalter and free it to
do its work among us. In this passionate essay Brueggemann
explores cases within the Psalms where limit expression gives
rise to candor, exuberance, memory, and hope.

In his explicitly theological essay Clint McCann discusses
the enemies in the Psalms, noting that the three lengthiest of
psalmic laments foreshadow the constant opposition Jesus
encountered during his life. Ironically, church people often
claim they have no enemies. McCann gently suggests that
faithfulness to the gospel puts us significantly out of step with
North American culture, which thus makes our culture our
enemy. McCann then explores the profound implications from
the prayers in the Psalms that commend a radical gratitude
especially important when confronting the culture of greed and
the pressure it exerts to define ourselves by what we are able to
purchase.

John Marks Hicks gives voice to a Psalmic genre largely
ignored in the suburban North American church: the communal
lament. While some peoples, including Ukrainians and African
Americans, have had a deeply textured expression of public
pain, many churches are filled with people disconnected from
triumphalist preaching and joy-focused worship. In the midst
of their personal anguish, believers often find no community
where worship acknowledges their reality. Hicks describes the
contrasting world of communal lament in the Psalms. He calls
preachers to make this genre part of the rhythm of the liturgical

experience, in sermon and song, to empower and transform the hurting and grieved.

The next chapter considers the New Testament's preaching of the Psalms. In dialogue with this tradition Ron Cox examines instances where we may profitably correlate the New Testament reading of the Psalms with our own. While these uses of the Psalms thwart some of our modern efforts, Cox observes constructive means where the New Testament uses the Psalms and offers specific ideas for our use. Following our New Testament guides, today's preaching should relate a word of God that refuses to be domesticated and makes uncommon demands of obedience, trust, and candor for all who will dare to engage.

The first section closes with Paul Scott Wilson's helpful schematic for reading the Psalms with a narrative plot. As a case study, Wilson contrasts ways three different preachers in different historical eras have looked outside the biblical text to reconstruct and reinterpret the third Psalm. In one era Augustine turned to Christ in the New Testament. In another time Calvin looked to David's life. In the current period Clinton McCann started with the life of his audience.[6] Wilson, in contrast, suggests an approach that uses the Psalms as "fictive plot", which is rooted in the biblical text and relates to both truth and fiction. Fictive plot honors the text by enhancing its features. To help preachers read the Psalms with imagination, Wilson sets out seven features of fictive plot, encouraging preachers to enroll their own creative efforts in using historical details and bending them to the form of the sermon's plot line.[7]

The sermons' connections with the essays are multifaceted and are given more specific nuance in each sermon's introduction. At times the sermons embody principles from the essays. For example, Brueggemann's call for "freshness" is created in the stunning opening of Mark Love's "Going to Church in the Psalms." Love creatively gives readers access to the oddness of the text with remarkable candor that opens the possibility of exuberance. On other occasions readers will detect specific interaction and reference to common texts and events. Jeff Christian's sermon from Psalm 103 takes to heart Brueggemann's treatise on the same passage. Christian's sermon identifies the limit experience of the listener before embodying a word of redemption. Christian's sermon creates a limit expression by imagining a world where despair is exchanged for compassion. As Brueggemann notes about Psalm 103, the guilt of sin is turned into the exuberance of God's mercy extended to his people.

In yet another connection with the book's sections, readers should note that this volume was written during the U. S. Senate Hearings and Pentagon investigation into administrative accountability for the brutal interrogation and inhumane prisoner abuse at Abu Ghraib. Walt Brueggemann's second essay[8] mentions this present evil as Mark Love's first sermon, with word and image, references the same cultural issue.[9] Both sermon and essay *start* with the world imagined in the Psalms *before* judging the present cultural evil. Theory is again given thoughtful and nuanced application

During the Rochester College Sermon Seminar one minister confided, "I am often teased by members of the congregation that I quote Walter Brueggemann way too often. I was once asked in a congregational meeting if Brueggemann might be available so that the church could eliminate the middle man." Readers of this volume will discover the work of Brueggemann and his colleagues to be generative and stimulating and thus find their own preaching enriched. The popularity and staying power of the essays and accompanying sermons in this volume will be the transcendent power revealed in the worlds imagined in the Psalms, their compelling call, judgment, and hope.

PART ONE

Essays on
Performing the Psalms

1

Psalms in Narrative Performance

Walter Brueggemann

I

The task of *preaching the Psalms* is exceedingly difficult, for the Psalms do not readily lend themselves to "being a text." Perhaps the Psalms were never intended in such a way. One can judge at the outset that because they are poetry often joined with music, performance in ways other than proclamation may be preferable. Beyond that, Psalms *too familiar* can hardly be heard with any freshness, and Psalms characteristically are *too*

- *odd* in many ways, too abrupt and disjunctive, too abrasive and filled with embarrassing passion, too linked to old cultural practices

- *generic,* and once we get the hang of them, they work only a small field of reality

- *remote* from us, awkwardly outmoded by being pre-scientific, pre-psychological, in general, pre-modern...alas!

At the outset, the preaching task must work as an antidote to these inherent problems, in order that the congregation can host these dangerous, subversive poems.

- Against excessive familiarity, the preacher must defamiliarize in order to show how remote from and challenging to our usual world of imagination is this rhetoric.

- In the face of Psalms too odd, the preacher's task is to create access to the oddness, to let the congregation see that what strikes us as odd in this material is matched by an oddness in our own life if and when we are able to step out of the world of illusion offered by the dominant ideologies of our culture. Those dominant ideologies make the world flat and safe. But, of course, in fact it is not like that in our lives. Thus, the oddity of the text, at first off-putting, can give access to the oddness in our own lives that the world teaches us not to notice.

- Against the impression that the Psalms are so generic, repetitious, and predictable that we can handle them casually, it is the preacher's attentive work to notice the particularity and peculiarity of each utterance. What appears to be generic is in fact "my utterance" or the utterance of some other speaking, intensely concerned agent for whom precision of utterance—so freighted with passion— is a life-or-death matter. It is, moreover, a life-or-death matter to be heard with presence, with attentiveness to nuance and cadence and detail.

- Against the notion that these Psalms are remote from us in their odd utterance, in their threat of vengeance, in their direct utterance of imperative, and in their capacity for doxology, it is the preacher's task to exhibit the truth that life that is fully human, life that is deeply faithful, is life precisely in such scale.

On all these counts the preacher, by repeated modeling, can embed in the congregation a poetic, imaginative dimension of dialogic life that turns obedience and candor into joy and doxology; and joy back to obedience and doxology back to candor.

II

In what follows, I suggest a strategy whereby the preacher may, with some intentionality, draw the congregation to life as it is uttered and imagined in the Psalter. In such a process, I suggest that the life of the congregation, over time, may be transposed by a practice of Psalmic dialogue into a communal existence of depth and deep staying power. The strategy I suggest is that the preacher must, with rich, playful imagination, transpose the Psalm into a narrative, in order to see that the Psalm in itself tells a story. The preacher must recover, or construct, the narrative situation in which the Psalm originated. In so doing, the preacher invites the congregation to resituate its life in this particular narrative so that it may come to see that this same narrative reading is being performed and re-performed in my life and in our life.

To this end, there are a myriad of little narratives–the narratives:

of a sheep
of a man on a journey
of a community in exile
that the many stars sang at creation
of a man just after adultery
etc.

These narratives are quite particular and concrete; they focus on one "critical incident" in the life of a community or a member of the community.

This myriad of little stories is based in, derives from, and contributes to a *meta-narrative* that in all of its rich diversity lays a singular claim on everyone in Israel. The meta-narrative that weaves in and through and stands under the little narratives asserts that the world is held in a sovereign, faithful purpose that is reliable, often invisible, and therefore not always trusted.

The *little narratives* and the sustaining *meta-narrative* share together the attestation that *YHWH is the central and decisive character* in the plot.

Given that characterization of the Psalter in terms of little narratives, meta-narrative, and the centrality of YHWH, it follows that the preaching task is the repeated re-performance of narrative thickness in particular ways that maximize the *crisis of narrative*. I use the term *crisis of narrative* to refer to the fact that this endless re-performance of narrative with this strong central character places in jeopardy all other narratives and invites to acute risk those who hear and embrace this narrative.

III

I want first, then, to explore the *crisis of narrative.* I begin by asking about the world of *thin narrative* within which this re-performance of Psalms occurs:

The narrative condition of the listening community may be one of the following:

1. There may be *no narrative* available to some. Last year at the Tate Museum in London, I saw an exhibit of "no narrative" portrayals. There was a particular sequence of paintings that struck me as uncommonly disclosing:

- *TV Room* by Paul Winstesky (1997) presented a modern, metallic pure TV room devoid of personal effects;

- *Overnight* by Michael Raedecker (1998) portrayed a darkened suburban ranch-style home that was silent and without signal of any human presence;

- *Room* by Lisa Melroy (1997) portrayed a Japanese kitchen with every gadget but no dynamism or relationship.

I take the sum of these three paintings that were exhibited in a series to portray a scene emptied of any human engagement. Nothing happens in the art; and nothing could happen, as there were no agents present. Such art portrays a world-without-story in which modern technique has expelled what might be human.

2. Some in the congregation may come with *bad narrative,* a narrative that in malevolent ways offers a future that is destructive and antihuman. Such bad narratives may arise from childhood destructiveness, rooted in silence, abuse, violence, or abandonment. Or it may arise from primary culture with the centrality of violence in the form of racism, sexism, consumerism, or militarism.

3. Some in the congregation may indeed have signed on to the biblical narrative in baptism or in confirmation or in church membership. But that biblical narrative has been so *ineptly*

construed in many places that it yields only a caricature of faith. Perhaps Mel Gibson's movie *The Passion of the Christ,* with its saturation of violence that bootlegs a particular theory of atonement, is an example of a poorly understood version of the biblical narrative.

4. Alongside *no narrative, bad narrative,* or *poorly construed narrative,* we recognize that in the congregation are those who have understood a faithful reading of the narrative. In our culture, however, even those with such a *narrative rightly construed* are pressed to the brink of distortion or abandonment and so depend in important ways on the recurring re-performance of the narrative to preclude loss of that narrative.

On all these counts, the congregation exhibits a readiness to attend to the re-performance of the narrative offered in the Psalter.

The narrative context of the congregation is not happenstance but in some measure is the outcome of the willful work of the *enemies of transformative narrative.* Indeed, the preacher and the congregation (and we) live amid powerful enemies of good narrative who seek to squelch the power of good narrative interaction and to void the presence and effect of the Key Character who always disrupts and creates crisis. We may identify three important enemies of good, transformative narrative:

Silence. We all know now that silence kills.[1] The silence may be imposed, or it may be an accidental moment in which there seems nothing to say because the time has become very thin with no available memory and no anticipated future.[2] The imposition of silence shrinks life and empties it of narrative playfulness.[3]

Technique. Contemporary technological capacity–given electronic capability–permits the redirection of all communication to one-dimensional transmission of information.[4] Such capacity, so it seems to me, renders communication thin and makes less likely playfulness, ambiguity, irony, or any of the puzzlements on which human interaction depends. For example, our newspaper issues a regular invitation on the obituary page to send "condolences" by e-mail. I doubt it. Rich, human interaction depends on rhetoric and discourse that are resistant to reductionism.

Ideology forecloses serious narrative interaction. Ideology yields no narrative; and if it ever would, it would be a narrative of legitimated violence in the interest of self-securing. The ideology of nihilism reduces all to commodity, as for example in the recent sale of body parts, but also, one suspects, in the recent invasion of Iraq, where an easy trade is made of bodies for oil. The ideology of the nation state substitutes hegemony for peace.

Thus, in readiness for the Psalter, I suggest that *no narrative, bad narrative,* and *narrative wrongly construed* serve the enemies of narrative—*silence, technique,* and *ideology*—all ending in violence.

IV

This analysis suggests that when the preacher prepares to re-perform little narratives and meta-narrative as testimony to Holy Character, the preacher enters a zone of immense danger and immense potential. The preacher evokes a crisis of narrative in which our previously held narrative may be exposed as inadequate and in which this new narrative is heard as subversive and generative. The narrative performance of the Psalms is characteristically a *counter-narration,* counter to *no narrative,* to *bad narrative,* and to *narrative poorly construed.* I suggest five elements in Psalmic performance as a grid in which the preacher and the congregation together may be uttered and heard to a life in God's world:

1. If the preacher's task is to re-narrate the life of the congregation and the world in which the congregation lives, we do no better than to begin with *the great narrative Psalms*—78, 105, 106, 136, and perhaps 135.[5]

The data of these renderings are fairly constant, focusing not only on the character of YHWH, but on YHWH's powerful, interventionist commitment to Israel.

Psalm 105 is a recital of miracles that constitute the memory of Israel. In this recital Israel fills its imagination with wondrous transformations of freedom and well-being, all of which are wrought as a gift by YHWH. The peculiar turn of verse 45 indicates the purpose of the recital:

> That they might keep his statutes
>   and observe his laws.
> Praise the LORD! (Ps. 105:45)

The entire recital, indeed the entire inventory of miracles, is "in order that" Israel should obey Torah. This narrative Psalm eventuates in ethics. People with this story are empowered to act differently in the world.

Psalm 106, intentionally placed back-to-back with Psalm 105, reiterates roughly the same data. Only this time, each mention of miracle is followed by an acknowledgement that Israel has violated the God of the miracle (vv. 6, 13, 28). The Psalm articulates a mismatch between YHWH's fidelity and Israel's treacherous infidelity. In the end, in verse 47, the Psalm moves to vigorous petition. The narrative functions, in this usage, to expose the disconnect between Israel and YHWH and to position Israel as a suppliant who cannot rely on autonomy but who can only count on YHWH who may yet, one more time, "save and gather."

Psalm 136, surely the greatest of these narrative recitals, again takes up the same narrative data. The definitive mark of this storytelling exercise, however, is that the second line of each verse of the Psalm offers the responsive litany, "The steadfast love of the Lord never ceases"(author's trans.). Israel's hermeneutical imagination can recognize that the entire *inventory of past miracles* serves to articulate *YHWH's abiding constancy.* The connection of the first line in its specificity and the second line in its routinization is not obvious, except in Israel's covenantal interpretation. But that, of course, is how narrative works. There is a thick connection between *the concrete* and *the ultimate* known only among the faithful. It is this connection that needs open-ended reiteration, lest the particulars cease to carry the larger freight of fidelity.

The outcome of this regular re-performance is a world that is unavailable except in the act of retelling.[6] Israel continues to retell this story because these memories are filled with and evoke astonishment. They testify to a world of surprise and subversive power. That astonishment abides in Israel and is found to be inexhaustible. We never finish with these remembered events, because the Holy One carried in the narrative regularly outdistances our explanatory capacity. We are left with dazzlement to which we must give continuing attestation.

We, with Psalm 105, are prepared for glad obedience.

We, with Psalm 106, are aware of our failure and voice petition with a resolve to give thanks.

We, with Psalm 136, are made to be and seen to be inhabitants of a world of deep fidelity.

The very recital subverts our more familiar worlds that have no grid for radical obedience, no move to petition, and so no cause for thanks, and in which fidelity is rare so that we must make our own way. The narratives mediate to us an alternative world and place our taken-for-granted world in doubt. Such is the task and opportunity of the preacher.

2. Within the framework of these large narratives, we may look more closely to see that many other Psalms, on a smaller scale, also offer a narrative. If we assume that a narrative plot characteristically assumes a *problematic* that moves toward *resolution,* then we may see that the Psalms regularly tell of such narrative implementation that moves from *trouble* to a conclusion of *joy, well-being, and thanks.*[7] I take my clue from Claus Westermann who, in reference to individual Songs of Thanksgiving, uses the phrase "narrative Psalms."[8] The speaker in the Psalm tells the tale of having moved from trouble to resolution or, as Westermann would say, from *plea* to *praise.* At the outset, such a narrative account derives from a specific, individual experience of transformation. In narrative re-performance, however, the initial experience becomes a model and paradigm through which subsequent narrative practitioners can relive their own experiences in the same reimagined way.

Psalm 107 provides four such brief narrative accounts of transformation. The first, in verses 4–9, is characteristic:

Some wandered in desert wastes,
> finding no way to an inhabited town;
hungry and thirsty,
> their soul fainted within them.
Then they cried to the LORD in their trouble,
> and he delivered them from their distress;
he led them by a straight way,
> until they reached an inhabited town.
Let them thank the LORD for his steadfast love,
> for his wonderful works to humankind.
For he satisfies the thirsty,
> and the hungry he fills with good things.
> (Ps. 107:4–9)

The plot of verses 4–9 moves in five elements:

a problematic
a cry to YHWH
an immediate divine response of rescue
a concrete expression of thanks
a generic doxology

Recurring though the plot may be, to the one who tells of her own experience this is not a recurring plot, but a once-in-a-lifetime miracle. It is, moreover, not different for those who later listen to this narrative account and draw it close to their own trouble, their own rescue, their own praise and thanks.

Verses 10–16, 17–22, and 23–32 offer three more cases of rescue narrated in turn–those from imprisonment, sickness, and storm at sea. The pattern is unvarying; the only difference is the description of the trouble and the concluding doxology that in each case circles back on the trouble. This drama is the characteristic rendering of this faith that pivots on *miracle* and ends in *thanks*. This scenario reflects the core of Israel's normative faith, a normative faith writ large in the Exodus narrative from the cry of Exodus 2:23–25 to the dance of Exodus 15:20–21 concerning the God who turns *pain* to *joy* (Jn. 16:20).[9]

If we take this narrative form as paradigmatic, we may notice how much of the Psalter participates in elements of this drama. Thus, prayers of *lament, complaint,* and *petition* reflect a statement of trouble and an anticipation of deliverance not yet enacted. On the other hand, if we focus on the concluding *thanks and doxology* in each scenario of Psalm 107, we may entertain the thought that the *hymns* of the Psalter reflect the latter part of the pattern, that is, celebration and exuberance at a new world enacted by the creator-sovereign God. Thus, most of the elements of the Psalter may be subsumed in this narrative structure, bringing both recurring predicament and recurring resolution into the rhetorical orbit of YHWH's good rule.

3. The scenario offered in Psalm 107 and in many of the Psalms are at best anonymous and, for the most part, generic. But the narrative is characteristically concrete and specific and resists any generalization. We are able to see in the canon of the Psalter itself, just as every preacher intuits, the felt need to *make the generic particular.* (We may assume an initial particularity, but in the traditioning process of the liturgy, that particularity has been in many cases superseded.) One strategic attempt at the recovery of the particular is evident in the *historical superscriptions* that have become attached to the Psalms in the oldest manuscripts. These superscriptions characteristically draw a generic Psalm close to the life of David, the presumptive voice of the Psalter, by linking the particular Psalms to the narrative account of David's life in the books of Samuel.

The best known of these is Psalm 51, with its familiar cadence of confession and repentance. The accent points of this Psalm are clear enough. The power of the Psalm, however, receives a jolt of new pertinence when the superscription is noticed:

> *A Psalm of David, when the prophet Nathan came to him, after he had gone in to Bathsheba.*

The superscription serves to position a generic Psalm of confession in the immediacy and particularity of the narrative of 2 Samuel 11–12. The indictment of the king accomplished by Nathan through a parable leads to a deep condemnation of David (2 Sam. 12:9–12), and a terse acknowledgement on David's part: "I have sinned against the LORD" (v. 13). The Psalm serves to elaborate that terse confession.

This narrative connection made by the superscription enables us to reread the Psalm with reference to the particularity of David and no doubt with a new poignancy toward all of our particularities that are marked by failure. Now the bid of the Psalm, "Have mercy on me," is not just a polite mantra, but an acknowledgment of deep need for a life that has been rendered miserable. Now the petition for a clean heart is the request of one with a failed heart. Now the asking for a restoration of joy comes from a deep dissent into joylessness, and the summons to a broken heart is from one whose heart had swelled in self-importance. The Psalm lingers long over the specificity of David; and as we keep the superscription in mind, we may readily move from David's particularity to our own particularity.

Less obviously, Psalm 34 is a song of thanksgiving for rescue. Reflective of the pattern that Westermann has discerned, this Psalmist can remember the previous situation of profound need and danger:

> I sought the LORD, and he answered me,
>   and delivered me from all my fears.
> Look to him, and be radiant;
>   so your faces shall never be ashamed.
> This poor soul cried, and was heard by the LORD,
>   and was saved from every trouble. (Ps. 34:4–6)

By the end of the Psalm, that context of danger has been overcome by the rescue of YHWH:

> Many are the afflictions of the righteous,
>   but the LORD rescues them from them all.
> He keeps all their bones;
>   not one of them will be broken.
> Evil brings death to the wicked,
>   and those who fate the righteous will be condemned.
> The LORD redeems the life of his servants;
>   none of those who take refuge
>   in him will be condemned. (Ps. 34:19–22)

Thus, the Psalm is a standard *drama of need and rescue.*

The superscription, however, draws the text close to David:

> *Of David, when he feigned madness before Abimelech, so that*
> *he drove him out, and he went away.*

The superscription refers to the narrative account of 1 Samuel 21:10–15, when David had fled from Saul to the Philistines. But what was to be a place of escape for David promptly became a place of danger, for the Philistine leader Achish recognized him. That recognition put David in jeopardy at the hands of the Philistines.

The value of the superscription and the narrative connection is that we read the Psalm with specificity. In doing so, it is remarkable to notice that the Psalm, in usual fashion, portrays the speaker—now David—as utterly without resources and dependent on YHWH. YHWH, moreover, is known to be powerful and utterly reliable and capable of rescue. But the interface of song and narrative does more than that. In the narrative account, David stays out of "harm's way" because of his own initiative, because of his competence as an actor, and because of his quick wits. In the narrative account David creates his own path of escape, and YHWH is never mentioned. The Psalm, remarkably enough, permits David (and us) to reread that narrative account of rescue toward YHWH. Now YHWH is credited with rescue.

The Psalm, taken by itself, is perhaps too clear and too neat. When the narrative of a would-be crazy man is stirred into the plot of the Psalm, we are able to see that *divine rescue* may take place in and through the *vagaries of human imagination and deception*. The superscription and the implied narrative enable us to read the Psalm with a thickness that is in, with, and under the familiar cadences of thanks.

We may then, given our general theme of narrative, reflect on the odd juxtaposition of *Psalms and superscriptions*. It is agreed in critical study that the superscriptions are not historically accurate. As Brevard Childs has shown, the superscriptions are rather interpretive clues for how the ongoing tradition has read the Psalms and wants them read.[10] The superscriptions are a scribal strategy whereby the now-lost particularity of the Psalms can be recovered in a second wave of narrative concreteness.

4. But of course, only a small number of Psalms have superscriptions that situate a Psalm concretely. My suggestion is that the preacher—because the task is to *re-narrate* the life of the congregation and each of its members through the Psalm—must by intuition and design introduce new superscriptions into the Psalter to draw the Psalm close to narrative specificity. In such a maneuver, the preacher may boldly replicate what the canonical process has done, for the biblical superscriptions are an act of imaginative imposition, just as will be the new superscriptions of the preacher. The exercise consists in asking, *Whose Psalm is this? Who might properly pray this Psalm today?* When those questions are asked, many connections may be made. Let me suggest some examples:

- Psalm 109 is an angry Psalm of vengeance in which an offended party petitions YHWH to destroy a human adversary. Once long ago, I asked a class who might pray this Psalm. Linda, a second career student, answered promptly, "It's perfectly obvious. This is the angry prayer of a woman who has just been raped." Now of course, taken with historical-critical carefulness, such a connection is without support. But intuitively, Linda had seen—perhaps experienced—that such a wound would evoke a prayer of rage that is barely sane. The Psalm has its decisive force in the congregation because of such intimate bodily violations that require powerful redress.

- Psalm 148 is a Psalm of creation that has all creatures praising the Creator. It is rather generic and lacks any specificity. But what if the superscription reads, "St. Paul's Church, Saline County, Missouri (my home church), the Sunday after the rain came after six months of drought"? That farming community is attentive to weather and depends on rain. But it also knows that rain is not given on demand or need. It is given in the mystery of creation. Thus, rain becomes a witness to the wonder of the creator; the congregation praises, but the congregation needs more participants for the doxology. And so it recruits other creatures (Ps. 148:3–10). The members of the community of praise stand in awe alongside cattle that will now have grass, squirrels that will have nuts, and sea monsters that wait in the saltwater for fresh flows of river water. All of these together crowd the trough of God's good food:

> The eyes of all look to you,
>   and you give them their food in due season.
> You open your hand,
>   satisfying the desire of every living thing.
> (Ps. 145:15–16)

The praise begins in rain but moves all through the seasons of seedtime and harvest, summer and winter, cold and heat.

- Psalm 46 is an articulation of the success and security of Jerusalem, perhaps in the wake of 701 B.C.E. and the deliverance of the city from the Assyrian siege. Behind such historicity is the more constant struggle of order against the wars of chaos. If on the other hand, we read forward, we will come to Luther's "Mighty Fortress," which is appropriated from the Psalm. Those uses, however, are still lacking in specificity for us. But consider this more contemporary superscription: "For the chapel at Columbia Theological Seminary on 9/12, the day after 9/11." Like many seminaries and many churches, our seminary had a long series of chapel services in the wake of 9/11. Without fail, the lead text every time was Psalm 46. Our usage did not think of Sennacherib or Luther; but we did, without verbalizing it, experience the ancient prehistoric threat of chaos. By our fingernails we held on to the ancient-contemporary utterance that the chaos so visible and so palpable could not outflank the powerful, ever-present God. We did not name the "city of God" that was made glad. Surely some imagined Washington, D.C., or New York City; but we likely, without too much precision, had in mind Atlanta or Decatur or Detroit or wherever our loved ones were thought to be in jeopardy. The Psalm was thereby drawn very close to the moment of narrated panic.

- Psalm 88 is a cry in the midst of absence. This is a speaker who has called and groaned and accused and summoned and petitioned, but with no divine response. Clearly the speaker is undelivered and will continue to assault the throne of mercy, seeking redress from the very God who has "put me in the depths of the Pit" (v. 6). It is not clear who speaks here. But a new superscription helps: "A Palestinian woman when a bomb–perhaps an Israeli bomb, perhaps a misdirected Palestinian bomb, she does not care which–has taken her beloved son." The loss she experiences is acute, and the pain is unbearable. She cannot have her son back; but she has a right to divine solace and comfort. And she receives none! She becomes an embarrassment to her community and is shamed by her neighbors, but she will not quit; she knows it is God's own neglect that has produced her sorry lot. She knows, and so do many other mothers in many places of violence who will join her cry once they see her and identify with the concreteness of her loss.

- Psalm 74 is a Psalm of grief and rage over the Babylonians' destruction of the temple in Jerusalem. This Psalm describes to YHWH in some detail the ruthlessness of destruction. Beyond that ancient destruction, Dietrich Bonhoeffer has famously connected this Psalm to Kristallnacht, that tragic, horrific night in November 1938 when the Nazis raided the Jewish communities, broke all the windows, and ravaged the properties. That destruction was a replication of the old Babylonian affront in Jerusalem. But the text does not end there. Imagine the superscription for the public funeral in Shelby County, Oklahoma, that reads:

"After the school bus accident that killed thirteen of our children":

> Your foes have roared within your holy place;
>   they set up their emblems there.
> At the upper entrance they hacked
>   the wooden trellis with axes.
> And then, with hatchets and hammers,
>   they smashed all its carved work.

They set your sanctuary on fire;
>   they desecrated the dwelling place of your name,
>   bringing it to the ground. (Ps. 74:4–7)

The ancient Jews in Jerusalem, the recent Jews in Berlin, the mothers and fathers in Shelby County, Oklahoma—all can use the same text. But they each use it specifically for their own crisis. They each grieve by retelling the violence.

The Psalm in each case becomes a bid to God to veto the brutality. In each case, in Jerusalem, in Berlin, and in Oklahoma, they remind God of God's immense power; God is not helpless in the face of violence:

Yet God my King is from of old,
>   working salvation in the earth.
You divided the sea by your might;
>   you broke the heads of the dragons in the waters.
You crushed the heads of Leviathan;
>   you gave him as food for the creatures of the
>   wilderness.
You cut openings for springs and torrents;
>   you dried up ever-flowing streams.
Yours is the day, yours also the night;
>   you established the luminaries and the sun.
You have fixed all the bounds of the earth;
>   you made summer and winter. (Ps. 74:12–17)

In each case—in Jerusalem, in Berlin, and in Oklahoma— the faithful address God in petition:

Rise up, O God, plead your cause;
>   remember how the impious scoff at you all day
>   long.
Do not forget the clamor of your foes,
>   the uproar of your adversaries that goes up
>   continually.
(Ps. 74:22–23)

What a word on the lips of the dismayed: Rise up! This is an Easter prayer, a bid for new life that depends on the mobilization of God's life-giving power. The faithful may pray this prayer generically but always out of a pit of a specific occasion of failed life.

Such superscriptions, the contemporary ones now added to the ancient ones, draw the classic, paradigmatic utterances of the Psalter close to lived reality. As this is done time after time, the congregation—in its song and prayer, in its protest and petition and praise—has its faith connected to real life in powerful ways. Over time the connection becomes thick and complex. To re-narratize the Psalms is to protest against vacuous generalization and to focus on concreteness wherein real people live real lives of agony and ecstasy.

V

Taken in this way Psalms offer real practices of faith in real contexts of life. The preacher's task is to invite the congregation to move from *no narrative* or *bad narrative* or *wrongly construed narrative* to these narratives that have long been found to be reliable. The preacher re-performs the text, and in so doing we find us also re-performing our lives with stunning force and accuracy. I cite two such re-performances:

Psalm 73 gives us a narrative account of a Torah believer who was almost talked out of Torah obedience. He noticed the rich and powerful who were autonomous, and he wanted to be like them:

> But as for me, my feet had almost stumbled;
>   my steps had nearly slipped.
> For I was envious of the arrogant;
>   I saw the prosperity of the wicked.
> For they have no pain;
>   their bodies are sound and sleek. (Ps. 73:2–4)

Just at the last moment, before he fell into destructive autonomy, he revised his life, remembered who he was, and remembered the God who had given him his life:

> I was stupid and ignorant;
>   I was like a brute beast toward you.
> Nevertheless I am continually with you;

you hold my right hand.
You guide me with your counsel,
and afterward you will receive me with honor.
Whom have I in heaven but you?
And there is nothing on earth
that I desire other than you.
(Ps. 73:22–25)

He had fallen into a world of commodity and only quite late did he come to see that he was created for a world of *communion* that resisted the thinness of *commodity*. Well, this is not my Psalm, likely not yours either. Except that it is the Psalm of every one of us who is privileged, who has opportunity for self-advancement, self-aggrandizement, self-serving, beguiled as we are by the big chances and the big banks and the big cars and the big lives that seem to be on offer. Let us imagine a superscription "for Howard, child of privilege, one year out of Harvard, a CPA with bonuses for hiring, almost empowered beyond recall, but stopped short by the quotidian truth of his life in a family of faith."

Or one other, Psalm 30. This is the voice of one who has been through the wringer and just made it. She tells how it went:

I was cocksure and self-satisfied, not unlike the parabolic man in Luke 12 who said to himself, "Eat, drink, and be merry":

As for me, I said in my prosperity,
"I shall never be moved."
By your favor, O LORD,
you had established me as a strong mountain.
(Ps. 30:6–7a)

But she found out that stuff happens in our lives in spite of our careful control:

You hid your face;
I was dismayed. (Ps. 30:7b)

She does not say what the trouble was. But we know. She got unexpectedly pregnant. She got breast cancer. She made a bad investment, and the light of God's countenance did not shine on her.

She prayed. She was, for all of that, still in the orbit of faith:

> To you, O Lord, I cried,
> and to the Lord I made supplication:
> "What profit is there in my death, if I go down to the Pit?
> Will the dust praise you?
> Will it tell of your faithfulness?
> Hear, O Lord, and be gracious to me!
> O Lord, be my helper!"
> (Ps. 30:8–10)

She threw herself on God's goodness. Being desperate, she bargained a little and reminded God how much God liked her voice of praise. She prayed; and then, after verse 10, there is a pause…until verse 11.

And then, without explanation, she affirms:

> You have turned my mourning into dancing;
> you have taken off my sackcloth and clothed me with joy. (Ps. 30:11)

We can never "explain" God's gift of newness. We receive it when it happens. She begins again, by the mercy of God, and is glad to offer that testimony.

So let us imagine a superscription. This is a real person attesting a lived life, so try this: "A song of Ella, child of privilege, driven close to failure, blessed by God's newness after the cancer." It is a song only for Ella, just hers. But we hear her song, and our own life seeps into it. Our life is like her life, because we also have been too self-confident. We also have known divine absence. We also have prayed and submitted and begged and borrowed. Some of us, not all of us, have been at it long enough to attest a turn to dancing. Generous Ella lets us sing with her. When we next say the Creed and mention "the communion of saints," we will remember Ella and all those who sing their songs that become, willy-nilly, our songs. The celebration of God's newness is never generic. It lives on the lips of specific witnesses who give concrete testimony that rings true as if it were our own.[11]

VI

So the preacher performs. She performs old texts. She performs with an eye, via the superscription, on the contemporary. It turns out, often, that the re-performance is of the narrative of our life and of my life. And out of that re-performance we notice:

1. The *fresh dramatic emergence of YHWH,* the key character in the plot, the one addressed, the one who speaks, the one known to be faithful, the one sometimes silent and absent, the one on whom are fixed all our hopes and our desperate needs.

2. The *fresh dramatic emergence of one's self,* alone but in the singing now with many brothers and sisters...Howard from Harvard; Ella from breast cancer; the preacher in Shelby County, Oklahoma; the people at St. Paul's in Saline County; and Linda after being raped. They all emerge. And we emerge from the new narrative that is peopled with prayer and praise, with trust and protest and need and comfort.

3. In this fresh dramatic emergence of God and self with brothers and sisters, I am newly aware of my life *situated in the matrix of this old, long, deep community,* summoned by many prayers and many songs, saints in obedience, sometimes saints in compromise, belated saints in weight of waywardness—all the great company that voices my life with utterances of candor and honesty, a compelling antidote to the contemporary powerful temptation toward hopeless thinness.

4. I hear the songs of Howard and Ella and Linda and many others, and I find my faith—not settled but generative, not boring but expectant—myself being *led beyond myself to new obedience and a new joy* that I could not have imagined for myself. All of this is made possible by this narrative engagement that makes all things possible that have been

precluded by old mantras and closed syllogisms and failed icons of self, all now fresh from the word!

5. Those who are able to resituate their lives in this counternarrative find themselves profoundly liberated. The capacity to *tell the truth* to the Holy One and to *hear hope* from the Holy One is indeed a transformative experience every time it happens.

6. This re-performance of this narrative through the script of the Psalter summons and empowers. But those who relive this narrative in the particularity of their own lives not only act, they sing. They sing endless praise, for life in this narrative becomes one long, loud, glad, exuberant, unresistant doxology. Below and behind and all around obedience, we are, in this re-performed narrative, "lost in wonder, love, and praise." In such singing, we are in the company of the abiding singing of the saints of the world to come (Rev. 4:10–11). That singing in the age to come, however, is already underway in this age among those for whom this narrative is re-performed. It is no wonder that life in this re-performed poetry culminates in such unrestrained praise; it is no wonder that the Psalter ends in the same way, as do our lives in the presence of God:

> Praise the LORD!
> Praise God in his sanctuary;
>   praise him in his mighty firmament!
> Praise him for his mighty deeds;
>   praise him according to his surpassing greatness!
> Praise him with trumpet sound;
>   praise him with lute and harp!
> Praise him with tambourine and dance;
>   praise him with strings and pipe!
> Praise him with clanging cymbals;
>   praise him with loud clashing cymbals!
> Let everything that breathes praise the LORD!
> Praise the LORD! (Ps. 150)

2

The Psalms as Limit Expressions

WALTER BRUEGGEMANN

I

The Psalms are strange, countercultural, and inherently subversive speech. Preachers and all who read these texts must take care not to tame them to familiarity. We tame the Psalms when we reduce them to praise songs. Episcopalians tame the Psalms by setting them to such nice music that one cannot notice what is being said. The scholarly tradition has its own ways of taming the Psalms. The whole work of Hermann Gunkel, Claus Westermann, and Erhard Gerstenberger has made clear that the Psalms are deeply disciplined in form. The form-critical enterprise has been an essential means to understand the Psalter under the restraints of social convention.[1]

In contrast, and this is the point I wish to make, the Psalms practice speech in ways that keep pushing the envelope beyond the already known to that which cannot be known until it is uttered. So the Psalms are always pushing up against the form and the restraint. It is best to allow the Psalms to be subversive enough to continue to surprise us in order that they may do their work amongst us.

The hymns can be rather stereotyped and are bodily acts of self-surrender. My Calvinist colleague, Erskine Clarke, was sitting in a Presbyterian church one Sunday when an outsider led the worship service. When the liturgist asked the people to raise their hands when they sang, Clarke's wife raised her hands. He said she was the first Clarke who got her hands above her ears in four hundred years. Some Evangelicals do bodily acts of surrender better than many in my tradition.

Yet laments, complaints, and protest use remarkable imagery with difficult and unexpected vocabulary. I draw that conclusion because laments are less stereotyped than praise, and praise requires less daring than Psalms of pain. For evidence, I've compiled a list of this kind of rhetoric from a few passages I've scanned:

- Psalm 52:2–"tongue as sharp as a razor" (author's trans.)
- Psalm 55:21–"speech smoother than butter"
- Psalm 56:8–"put my tears in your bottle"
- Psalm 57:1–"shadow of your wings"
- Psalm 57:4–"teeth are spears" and "tongues [are] sharp swords"
- Psalm 58:8–"like the snail that dissolves into slime"
- Psalm 59:6–"howling like dogs"

So, the gladness-telling of hymnic Psalms is more stereotyped, but the renderings of praise are bodily acts of letting one's body soar beyond control in self-surrender.[2]

II

This odd rhetoric of discipline and extravagance leads me to appeal to Paul Ricoeur's category of "limit expression."[3] In his *Essays on Biblical Interpretation,* Ricoeur identifies five genres of biblical testimony that are used to redescribe reality in evangelical terms:

1. Prophetic Discourse
2. Narrative Discourse
3. Prescriptive Discourse
4. Wisdom Discourse
5. Hymnic Discourse[4]

Ricoeur's talk of the five modes of testimony occurs in a different place than his discussion of limit expressions, but my hunch is that Ricoeur would say that all of these modes of testimony in the Bible are in fact limit expressions. Ricoeur uses a series of words and phrases to characterize limit expression, by which he means words and phrases that push one to the extremity of human experience. Thus, Ricoeur describes limit expressions:

- enacting total commitment, without accommodation to other claims
- odd
- capable of disclosure
- extravagant
- eruptions of the unheard
- redemptive
- of unusual significance
- extremities
- the extraordinary in the ordinary

Church rhetoric should never be ordinary, not even ordinary as church rhetoric. Ricoeur, quoting Robert Funk, says that limit expression "ruptures the tradition and permits a glimpse of another world through the cracks."[5] The Psalms permit a glimpse of another world through the cracks. In his chapter in this volume, Clint McCann opens the crack to help us see the world of gratitude in an ocean of greed. So being saved—or being baptized, or coming to Christ, or whatever language one uses—is moving into this world we've only glimpsed through rhetoric.

Ricoeur concludes that limit expressions "preserve symbols from idolatry."[6] The rhetoric of such utterances resists thinness and flatness and refuses safe, managed life. Such utterances give access to the deep, conflicted places where holiness is at work for transformative healing and newness.

Ricoeur takes parables as his primary example of limit expression. By parable he means that which has inexhaustible meaning.[7] There is always more and more and more. Occasionally when Jesus tells a parable, his disciples ask for clarification. Jesus in his Southern dialect responds, "Y'all think about that." Limit expression moves beyond management. With limit expression we will always return to an utterance to learn again.[8]

Limit expression is a contrast to conventional speeches of closure that end discussion, give certainty, and button everything down. Speech of closure is the right speech for control, management, and administration. Speech of closure writes memos that are unambiguous. But you can't live by memos. Such speech of closure is not adequate speech for being human, for to be human means to have an openness to mystery, to expect newness, and to yield to the gift of transformation.

Limit *expression,* says Ricoeur, gives access to limit *experience,* to those dimensions of lived reality that defy our habitual settlements. We experience this daily, but unless we have rhetoric for it, we cannot fully experience our experience. We will flaunt it and experience it as ordinary and routine. These "limit experiences" may be positive experiences of joy and elation. The quintessential example is the birth of a baby, when we are overwhelmed by inexplicable gift. Or limit experiences may be negative experiences of hurt, loss, grief, and anger. But in both the positive and the negative, the deep recesses of genuine humanness reside. Ministers, I wish you to observe, have access to this stuff like no one else.

But, says Ricoeur, we have no effective access to limit *experiences* unless we have available limit *expressions.* Without utterances of dangerous probe, we are denied access to our deep humanness. We are consequently fated to live in the safe middle ground that is cut off from the extremities of our life where our God-given image is most on exhibit. When we settle for safe middle ground, we are to some extent numbed to the dangerous, wondrous parts of our life wherein we are most like the dangerous, wondrous creator God who has called us into being. My thesis in this chapter is that the pulpit may be the last place in U.S. society for limit expressions.

I argue that the Psalter is the most tried, tested, and true collage of limit expression in the history of humanity. And it has been entrusted to us. What an amazement! Thus, I propose that the preaching of the Psalms is an act of offering limit expressions through which the congregation is given to its limit experiences, which are otherwise, in our culture, mostly inaccessible. In what follows, then, I will consider some ways in which the Psalms may be practiced as limit expression.

III

This practice of limit expression that gives access to limit experience is important because such practice and such access are indispensable for the maintenance of covenantal, dialogic humanness.[9] This practice of limit expression is so difficult because there are indeed willful, determined enemies of limit expression who do not want there to be access to limit experience, because such practice and such access characteristically call the status quo into question and hold potential of making all things new.

I suggest that the re-performance of dialogic narrative as limit expression is always "in the face" of such resistance. The programmatic work of Emanuel Levinas articulates nicely this deep dispute in the two terms of his crucial book title, *Totality and Infinity*.[10] By *totality,* Levinas means a closed system of symbols that offers a world completely contained, controlled, and domesticated. In contrast, by *infinity,* he means a world and a life that is endlessly opened in newness that is yet to unfold. Thus, I propose that *infinity* is practiced in limit expression, whereas *totality* is accomplished by the enemies of limit expression, of which I here name four candidates:

1. **Absolute truth** is an enemy of limit expression, whether it takes the form of dogma, morality, or any political or economic claim that imagines the final answers are already in.[11] Such posture leaves room for no surprise or for the reconfiguration of reality through fresh utterance. In the church, as outside the church, such absolutism takes two highly visible forms, conservatism of an authoritarian kind and liberalism of a strident, shrill variety. The effect of such absolutism always silences dissent and excommunicates those who do not consent, submit, and conform.

2. **Ideology** is only a step further than absolute truth, the practice of taking a part of truth and making it the whole, most often the part that supports a self-interest. Ideology imagines that it has a monopoly on truth and must perforce condemn as heretical or treasonable all those who think otherwise. Paul O'Neill, in his exposé of the government, concludes, "Ideology comes out of feelings and it tends to

be non-thinking...Ideology is a lot easier because you
don't have to know anything or search for anything. You
already know the answer to everything. It's not penetrable
by facts. It's absolutism."[12]

In this deeply determined practice of absolutism, all
alternatives are silenced. Eventually, all those who do not
conform are excommunicated, that is, declared not to
exist.

3. **Technology,** as Alvin Gouldner and Jacques Ellul have
shown, is indeed a practice of ideology.[13] Technology as a
way of defining relations and shaping reality is quick to
identify the ideological dimension of all else and easily
imagines itself to be neutral and noncommittal with, as
Gadamer says, "it's bias against bias."[14] But of course, what
technology does is to reduce everything to one option, an
option that characteristically tilts toward and advantages
those who are presently powerful and privileged.

Technological communication, in its electronic modes,
cannot entertain nuance or depth or ambiguity, and so
must exclude the rich playfulness that belongs to real
communication. Consequently, I have wondered if it is
possible to send "notes of condolence" by electronic means,
or is it obscene to try to do so in a medium that defies the
message? What about love letters? or prayers? or, for that
matter, any communication that silences the rich and
inscrutable underneathness of genuine human interaction?

4. I am not sure, but I wonder if excessive utilization of drugs
and excessive attentiveness to **body care** are in fact enemies
of limit expression. I do not refer to "drug pushers" and
"drug traffic," but to consumer goods of body care of a
thousand kinds, all of which seek to make our bodily
existence immune to pain, hurt, discomfort, distortion, or
the ugliness wrought by the normal hazards of life. The
"totalism" of such a social practice is to produce bodily
existence that is in daily, quotidian denial of the erosions
of mortality.[15] And, of course, the exotic, expensive forms
of medical adventure into the prolongation of life

constitute a more dramatic form of silencing the creature-liness to which we are destined.

I, of course, take in a great deal of territory to label as totalism all that includes absolute truth, ideology, technique, and body care of an exotic kind. Without disputing detail, I list these as rough representatives of the effort to keep life "thin" and without the complexity of the risk and reality that belongs to human living. The effort to silence reduces the danger of life but also curbs the huge, inscrutable potential of humanness.

I propose that such silencing totalism is inherently idolatrous. Such silencing imagines a fixed, closed, settled, thin, safe, reduced existence that has as its center, if indeed it has a center, a fixed object that makes it possible for life to be a monologue. Monologue always turns out to be idolatry. I mean to say that every major ideological force, including the church, becomes a cottage industry for idolatry. But of course, such idolatrous fixity is not new. Israel already knew about the temptations to totalism that precluded an open future. Consider Psalm 115, and when you read *idol,* think *monologue.*

> Their idols are silver and gold,
>   the work of human hands.
> They have mouths, but do not speak;
>   eyes, but do not see.
> They have ears, but do not hear;
>   noses, but do not smell.
> They have hands, but do not feel;
>   feet, but do not walk;
>   they make no sound in their throats.
> Those who make them are like them;
>   so are all who trust in them. (Ps. 115:4–8)

In this Psalm, verse 8 is especially poignant. It is, of course, troubling enough to have such an "ultimate loyalty" that does not move, speak, or change. The real risk, however, is that those who worship such fixity become like that which they worship...fixed, unable finally to move, speak, receive gift, notice newness, or change: "Those who make them are like them; so are all who trust in them."

IV

The news of the gospel is that such fixity is precisely countered by the God who makes all things new. The task of preaching is to be the point person in the enactment of infinity that counters totalism. The alternative of infinity against totalism is accomplished by refusing monologue of either absolute authority (as in ideology) or absolute autonomy (as in exotic body care) by performing and re-performing dialogue that breaks every silence. The preacher's task is to verbalize limit expression that gives access to limit experience, the very limit experience that the enemies of limit want not to experience.

The Psalms are among the most poignant scripts for dialogic infinity that we have. Preaching, then, is to authorize dialogic practice in the congregation that gives access to our rich creatureliness that is precluded in our cultures of silence. The meeting of the Christian congregation is where we do battle for our humanness.

Think about how this happens in your preaching. Limit expression gives people access to limit experience. After church you get thanked for all sorts of things you did not say. And you get blamed for all sorts of things you did not say because this kind of speech opens people to the stuff that is going on here about which they do not know. Think, then, of preaching the Psalms as giving people access to the parts of their lived experience that they have not yet experienced or had access to.

I want now to mention five examples of such limit expressions in the Psalms that are counter to idolatrous silence. These five cases are typical and representative and provide, in my judgment, a taxonomy of preaching in a culture bent on silence.

The first case: **Psalm 44 and the limit of candor.**[16] Psalm 44 is a most outrageous Psalm, and we may be dazzled that it made the canon at all. The Psalm has three parts. The first verses (1–8) review the memory of YHWH's many miracles and state that the present generation continues to trust YHWH on the basis of remembered miracles. The last four verses (23–26) act as a conclusion and issue demanding, imperative petitions to YHWH that YHWH should act: "Rouse yourself"; "Awake"; "Rise up"; "Redeem."

Our interest, however, turns on the middle verses (9–22), which is a wholesale *attack* on YHWH as the one who has abused and maltreated Israel. This part of the Psalm begins with the particle *'aph,* or in some manuscripts, *'ak.* Either way, the particle is an abrupt interjection that reverses rhetorical direction from the preceding verses. For eight verses the psalm says, "You are such a wonderful and miraculous God." And then, in verse 9, "*yet.*" Verse 9 moves from *trust* to *accusation,* rendered in the NRSV as "yet."

Then proceeds a series of direct accusations about "you YHWH," and what "you" have done to us:

> Yet **you** have rejected us and abased us,
>   and have not gone out with our armies.
> **You** made us turn back from the foe,
>   and our enemies have gotten spoil.
> **You** have made us like sheep for slaughter,
>   and have scattered us among the nations.
> **You** have sold your people for a trifle,
>   demanding no high price for them.
> **You** have made us the taunt of our neighbors,
>   the derision and scorn of those around us.
> **You** have made us a byword among the nations,
>   a laughingstock among the peoples.
> All day long my disgrace is before me,
>   and shame has covered my face. (Ps. 44:9–15)

In some churches, following the reading of the Scripture the congregation says, "This is the word of the Lord. Thanks be to God." You don't want to say that after Psalm 44.

This accusation in Psalm 44 is balanced in verses 17–19 with a statement of Israel's uncompromising loyalty to YHWH, thus exposing YHWH as the faithless one in this relationship. In the NRSV (though not in the Hebrew), this section offers two more "yets":

> All this has come upon us,
>   **yet** we have not forgotten you,
>   or been false to your covenant.
> Our heart has not turned back,
>   nor have our steps departed from your way,

> **yet** you have broken us in the haunt of jackals,
>   and covered us with deep darkness. (Ps. 44:17–19)

This middle section of the poem is astonishing. First, it reverses the trust of verses 1–8. But second, it becomes the ground of petition at the end. Israel attests that YHWH has been fickle, but continues to believe that YHWH can be summoned yet again to fidelity, YHWH's fidelity being Israel's only hope for the future. This middle section of the poem attests that Israel's candor about its life knows no limit. One can say anything. Israel will speak the truth, because failure to speak the truth will result in denial and grudging, paralyzing submission.

Psalm 44 is indeed an extreme case, a genuine limit expression. This Psalm would not be used often, but saved for special times of acute negation. We may imagine its superscription, because it has none in the text:

> The prayers in Coventry at the bombing;
> The prayers in Dresden at the firebombing;
> The prayers in Hiroshima with the bomb;
> The prayers in Manhattan on 9/11.

The Psalm poses the question, What shall we do with unspeakable alienation wrought by violence? Too much our current practice is to hug and grow romantic. But Israel will not settle for that because it will not relinquish its conviction that YHWH is indeed Lord and governor, and so must give answer. Thus, the Psalm is a dread-filled acknowledgement, anticipating Job, that the world is indeed governable and governed, and the governor must answer. This Psalm, and some with lesser nerve, model the extreme limit of candor. Does your church know that Psalm 44 is in the Bible?

Tania Oldenhage, in *Parables For Our Time,* reflects on "lament rhetoric" in relationship to the Holocaust and "the face of evil."[17] She cites the work of Terrence Des Pres, *The Survivor,* concerning limit rhetoric in the death camps.[18] I do not trivialize the death camps, but suggest that they are an extreme model of many other lived realities in the face of evil. Candor is a gift and permit of faith that precludes denial and draws God's own life into the arena of evil. The practical function of this Psalm and others like it is to give permission and authority to the congregation to practice candor in its own life in the presence of God.

As I wrote this essay, the Iraqi prison scandal had begun to unfold. There is nobody left in the United States to be honest about what is happening to us, except ministers. And the Psalms are our script. It is all there. As Calvin said, the Psalms are the anatomy of the soul. So think of your preaching as Anatomy 101, about who we are and how we are.

The second case: **Psalm 103 and the limit of exuberance.** More familiar and easily credible to us are hymns of praise that exhibit Israel when it cedes its life over to YHWH in trustful abandonment. These hymns are so familiar that we do not notice the exaggerated readiness of Israel to engage in shameless public acts of glad self-surrender.

Psalm 103 is familiar, and I will not take up the Psalm in its fullness, but will refer to only a few matters in this wondrous limit articulation. In the body of the Psalm, we may note two narrative forays. First, in verses 6–14, the Psalm deals with the problem of sin and finds the divine antidote to sin in YHWH's parental compassion and fidelity:

> The LORD is merciful and gracious,
>> slow to anger and abounding in steadfast love.
> He will not always accuse,
>> nor will he keep his anger forever.
> He does not deal with us according to our sins,
>> nor repay us according to our iniquities.
> For as the heavens are high above the earth,
> so great is his steadfast love toward those who fear him;
> as far as the east is from the west,
>> so far he removes our transgressions from us.
> As a father has compassion for his children,
>> so the LORD has compassion for those who fear him.
> for he knows how we were made;
>> he remembers that we are dust. (Ps. 103:8–14)

Everything turns on YHWH's fidelity and compassion that lives reliably beneath sin and is an adequate counter to sin.

Second, the Psalm reflects on finitude, mortality, and death and finds divine fidelity to be a durable antidote to human intransigence:

> As for mortals, their days are like grass;
>   they flourish like a flower of the field;
> for the wind passes over it, and it is gone,
>   and its place knows it no more.
> But the steadfast love of the LORD is from everlasting to everlasting
>   on those who fear him,
>   and his righteousness to children's children,
> to those who keep his covenant
>   and remember to do his commandments.
> (Ps. 103:15–18)

Thus, the Psalmist pushes our awareness toward the twin realities of human risk: guilt and death. The Psalm is honest about both, but nonetheless joyous in the face of that honesty, precisely because it can imagine a good resolution.

This Psalm is an example of a limit expression of *candor* "concerning guilt and death" that is turned to *exuberance*. Unlike so-called praise hymns, this hymn of praise is down and dirty in human problematics and does not flinch. It does, moreover, have a dramatic and narrative development so that the speaker of the Psalm moves to a new place because of the reality of God. This capacity for dramatic development and narrative movement is unlike so-called praise hymns that simply stay in one place and endlessly repeat.

These two narrative realities of *sin forgiven* and *death enveloped by mercy* are preceded in the Psalm by a summary doxology wherein Israel gathers its long conviction that YHWH's transformative verbs overwhelm Israel's life and, more generically, the human predicament:

> who forgives all your iniquity,
>   who heals all your diseases,
> who redeems your life from the Pit,
>   who crowns you with steadfast love and mercy,
> who satisfies you with good as long as you live

so that your youth is renewed like the eagle's.
(Ps. 103:3–5)

The whole "finally" is bracketed by a summons to join the limit speech of exuberance:

Bless the LORD, O my soul,
   and all that is within me,
   bless his holy name.
Bless the LORD, O my soul,
   and do not forget all his benefits...
Bless the LORD, O you his angels,
   you mighty ones who do his bidding,
   obedient to his spoken word.
Bless the LORD, all his hosts,
   his ministers that do his will.
Bless the LORD, all his works,
in all places of his dominion,
Bless the LORD, O my soul. (Ps. 103:1–2, 20–22)

At the beginning of the Psalm the speaker gathers the speaker's own life that is mobilized fully in candor and exuberance toward YHWH. But then, in the concluding verses of the Psalm, the speaker moves well beyond self; now also summoned to join the doxological celebration are angels and mighty ones and all the host of heaven. All works, all creatures, in all places! Finally, in the last line, there is a return to the first line about the self who is now marked doxologically amid a doxological world of YHWH's glad creatures. The reality of YHWH's transformative fidelity requires that all creatures in heaven and on earth should sing together. The doxology is a feeble human attempt at limit utterance that may match the divine act of limit gift. In such a field of rhetoric, it is not necessary to mumble about human reality, because divine reality actively overwhelms. There is so much about which to sing!

The third case: **Psalm 77 and the limit of memory.** Israel is sustained by its memory and never suffers amnesia...but it sometimes comes close to amnesia.[19] Psalm 77 is a deep probe into personal trouble. In verses 1–10, the speaker is preoccupied with self; it is all about "me":

In the day of **my** trouble **I** seek the Lord;
in the night **my** hand is stretched out without wearying;
my soul refuses to be comforted.
I think of God, and **I** moan;
I meditate, and **my** spirit faints...

"Has God forgotten to be gracious?
Has he in anger shut up his compassion?"
And **I** say, "It is **my** grief
that the right hand of the Most High has changed."
(Ps. 77:2–3, 9–10)

The Psalmist pushes to the limit the centrality of the self. In that very rhetorical preoccupation, however, the speaker discovers that there is no resolution of trouble by self-reference. Indeed, it is so characteristic in Israel that even with self-preoccupation, the self must address YHWH.

Then in verse 11, the Psalm makes a characteristic move to the past that is permeated by YHWH, so that the self is repositioned in a thick communal memory. It becomes clear in this drastic turn from self to communal past that the power of memory is deep; Israel's rhetoric can probe that past, but it can never touch the bottom of it:

I will call to mind the deeds of the LORD;
I will remember your wonders of old.
I will meditate on all your work,
and muse on your mighty deeds.
Your way, O God, is holy.
What god is so great as our God?
You are the God who works wonders;
you have displayed your might among the peoples.
With your strong arm you redeemed your people,
the descendants of Jacob and Joseph.
(Ps. 77:11–15)

The language of the Psalm is filled with the rich vocabulary of miracle...deeds, wonders, work, mighty deeds, wonders, might, redeemed. Then in verse 16, the Psalm becomes specific and speaks in detail about the defining, transformative miracle of exodus:

When the waters saw you, O God,
> when the waters saw you, they were afraid;
> the very deep trembled.
The clouds poured out water;
> the skies thundered;
> your arrows flashed on every side.
The crash of your thunder was in the whirlwind;
> your lightnings lit up the world;
> the earth trembled and shook.
Your way was through the sea,
> your path, through the mighty waters;
> yet your footprints were unseen.
You led your people like a flock
> by the hand of Moses and Aaron. (Ps. 77:16–20)

The phrasing is familiar, voicing testimony to YHWH's paradigmatic intervention of power. It strikes one that the Psalm at the end does not circle back to the speaking self. It does not explicitly connect the exodus and the self. Rather, the connection is implied and understood in Israel. The speaking self has gone the limit of communal memory, and in the process has taken the communal memory as the resolution of the self. All concern about "my trouble" and "my [fainting] spirit" is now repositioned in the thick limit of Israel's standard credo recital. Israel knows that this is as close as we will ever come to the resolution of the self.

The fourth case: **Psalm 96 and the limit of hope.** Israel knows full well that the world is out of kilter. In response to that awareness, Israel meets regularly in an extreme liturgical act of hope, a waiting for a coming divine resolution. For that occasion of communal waiting, the temple staff has produced a new anthem of limit:

O sing to the LORD a new song;
> sing to the LORD, all the earth.
Sing to the LORD, bless his name;
> tell of his salvation from day to day.
Declare his glory among the nations,
> his marvelous works among all the peoples.
(Ps. 96:1–3)

The subject of the new song is YHWH who, it is not doubted, can right the world.

The substance of Israel's hope, voiced in monarchal rhetoric, is that the true King-Creator will come soon and override all chaos. Scholars debate whether the coming of YHWH is understood as a cultic epiphany or, in more narrow Calvinist understanding, as an eschatological event.[20] But in the actual utterance of the Psalm, such critical distinctions are not operative or important. Thus, Israel's extremity of hope is that the creation will be righted by the powerful action of the Creator:

> Say among the nations, "The LORD is king!
>   The world is firmly established; it shall never be moved.
>   He will judge the peoples with equity." (Ps. 96:10)

Notice what a huge affirmation this is. Indeed, I have come to think that Psalm 96:10 is the quintessential statement of the gospel in all of Old Testament scripture. This is the ground of Israel's hope. It is, moreover, the ground of the Oracles Against the Nations that are to appear in the prophetic books that assert YHWH's sovereignty over all the centers of power in the world.[21] Our usual creedal confession in the church puts the Creator only at the beginning, as though the work of the Father were simply to start the world. Israel's rhetoric of doxology, however, puts the Creator at the culmination of well-being. It is the ultimate coming of the Creator that is the hope of Israel, that the world eventually will be righted according to the intention of the Creator.

The consequence of such affirming joy among all the creatures is that they rejoice that the world will be made right:

> Let the heavens be glad, and let the earth rejoice;
>   let the sea roar, and all that fills it;
>   let the field exult, and everything in it.
> (Ps. 96:11–12a)

This is an act of hope that is pertinent to everyone:

- It concerns the sea, because the chaos of water pollution will end.

- It concerns the field, because chemical contamination fertilizer will cease.
- It concerns the trees, because deforestation will stop.

As a consequence, all sing. All clap. All celebrate what will be soon. There is no need to work out a "proper" eschatology. It is enough to engage at the extreme limit of imaginable possibility:

> Then shall all the trees of the forest sing for joy
>> before the LORD; for he is coming,
>> for he is coming to judge the earth.
> He will judge the world with righteousness,
>> and the peoples with his truth. (Ps. 96:12b–13)

All will be well. This is not play-acting. Such limit utterance is engagement with deep issues, in this case a glad assertion that chaos is penultimate and cannot prevail against the steady resolve of the Creator.

The fifth case: **Psalm 112 and the limit of new humanness.** Consider the sum of such limit utterances cited above:

- Candor that moves to demand (Ps. 44)
- Exuberance when death and guilt are resolved (Ps. 103)
- Memory that repositions the self (Ps. 77)
- Hope that submits chaos to God's coming rule (Ps. 96)

It is important to ponder what it is like to be regularly in a speech practice of this sort. It is important to imagine the kind of human personhood made possible by such nurture and such testimony. Psalm 112 is a portrayal of a person who is generated by such practice; in this case, the portrayal is expressed in masculine patriarchal fashion, but we may readily transpose it beyond those categories.

- Such a person is "lucky":

> Praise the LORD!
>> Happy are those who fear the LORD,
>> who greatly delight in his commandments. (Ps. 112:1)

- Such a person, a product of limit speech, is prosperous and has the wherewithal to be generous and merciful:

Their descendants will be mighty in the land;
> the generation of the upright will be blessed.
Wealth and riches are in their houses,
> and their righteousness endures forever.
They rise in the darkness as a light for the upright;
> they are gracious, merciful, and righteous.
(Ps. 112:2–4)

- Such a person invests in the community in generosity and is committed to justice for the vulnerable:

It is well with those who deal generously and lend,
> who conduct their affairs with justice. (Ps. 112:5)

- Such a person is unflappable and has a stable capacity for well-being in the face of adversity:

For the righteous will never be moved;
> they will be remembered forever.
They are not afraid of evil tidings;
> their hearts are firm, secure in the LORD.
Their hearts are steady, they will not be afraid;
> in the end they will look in triumph on their foes.
(Ps. 112:6–8)

An unflappable Episcopal bishop served in Canada. The diocese was sued and lost everything. The next day at a press conference the bishop said, "Well, if we get a table, a cup, and a book, we're back in business." It was one of the most moving testimonies of our times.

- Such a person cares for the neighbor in generative ways:

They have distributed freely, they have given to the poor;
> their righteousness endures forever;
> their horn is exalted in honor. (Ps. 112:9)

The outcome of such speech is, it is here attested, a radically different kind of humanness. It is the product of preaching that dares to go to the extremities to probe the mysteries of human life. Our society does not want this to happen. Our society fears that people will stop going to the mall and become dangerous subversives. We ministers, however, must repent of taming and domesticating the Psalter and allow it to do its work amongst us.

V

So, dear preachers, ponder life with these speech practices made available in the community. And then think about the immense loss where such speech is not practiced, such speech that gives permit and authority beyond a safe middle ground.

- Take away the *candor* of Psalm 44 and then settle for *denial.*
- Take away the *exuberance* of Psalm 103 and then settle for the *anguish of guilt* and the *weight of mortality.*
- Take away the *memory* of Psalm 77 and continue to wallow in *self-preoccupation.*
- Take away the *hope* of Psalm 96 and *let chaos become definitional.*

The outcome of such default in language will be selves that are turned in on themselves and against neighbor, sure to be devoured by anxiety.

I propose, then, our continued thinking about these claims:

- That the preacher is designated precisely to practice limit expressions in order that our humanness should not shrivel to consumers and patriots.
- That the script for such practice of limit expression is the Psalter, with its daring extravagance toward every limit of the project of creation.
- That the act of preaching is one of the few venues left for such regular sustained speech in our society; people still know that we "talk funny" and that we talk textually in the church as almost nowhere else.
- That such practice of limit expression is the most radical social action in which the church can participate. Such speech is an antidote to technological flatness, to consumer self-preoccupation, and to military violence.
- That in a congregation where such speech is practiced in sustained ways, there will be ample impetus for generosity in stewardship and energy for neighborly mission.

Everything depends on the congregation and its sense of difference. That difference derives from difference in speech, and that depends on the imaginative lips of the preacher, funded by these texts that defy closure.

3

Greed, Grace, and Gratitude

*An Approach to Preaching
the Psalms*

J. CLINTON McCANN JR.

My approach in this essay is explicitly theological. In its most basic sense, theology means thinking about God. So, as I interpret the Psalms for preaching, I am constantly looking for a word from and about God and God's will for the world. More specifically, my working definition of theology is borrowed from David Tracy, who suggests that doing theology means thinking about religion culturally and thinking about culture religiously.[1] Or, as I like to paraphrase Tracy, theology is thinking about God and God's claim on the world in the context of where we find ourselves every day.

As contemporary North Americans, where we find ourselves every day is in the midst of an extremely affluent culture in which greed is pervasive. The singing group Sweet Honey in the Rock has a song entitled "Greed (A Sermonette)," in which they suggest that they are "trying to find a way to talk about greed."[2] In a real sense, this essay is doing the same thing, in conversation with the book of Psalms. In the first section, which focuses on the prayers in the Psalms (usually known as the laments or complaints), I shall suggest that attending to the pervasive reality of the enemies in the Psalms can serve to put us in touch with contemporary socioeconomic arrangements that oppose God's will for the world—in short, I shall suggest that the prayers in the book of Psalms can teach us that greed is to be viewed as an enemy of God and of God's people. In the second section, which focuses on praise in the Psalms, I shall suggest that the antidote to rampant greed is the gratitude fostered by attending to the praise and thanksgiving found in the book of Psalms.

In the Presence of My Enemies: The Prayers for Help in the Psalter

Although it has often been overlooked, a regular feature of the prayers in the Psalter is the presence of the psalmists' *enemies,* or as they are also called (NRSV): "the wicked," "the foes," "the bloodthirsty," "evildoers," "workers of evil," "pursuers," "fools," "hypocrites," "adversaries," "false witnesses," "malicious witnesses," "ruffians," "wrongdoers," "those who seek my life," "the proud," "the arrogant," "assailants," "the insolent," "the ruthless," and sometimes metaphorically, "bulls," "dogs," and "lions." In fact, in Books I and II of the Psalter (Pss. 1–72), where the prayers for help are concentrated, every psalm that is generally categorized as a prayer for help (or a lament/complaint—there are forty-six of them) has some reference to the enemies, with the possible exceptions of Psalm 4 (which does, however, mention people who "love vain words, and seek after lies"), Psalm 51 (in which the psalmist is his or her own worst enemy, and which does mention "transgressors" and "sinners"), and Psalm 62 (in which the enemies are implied by way of a description of their activities—"assail a person" and "batter your victim"). By any accounting, therefore, the enemies in the book of Psalms are pervasive, if not omnipresent. And what is more, the psalmists several times complain that even their apparent friends, companions, and neighbors have become their opponents (see Pss. 38:11; 41:9). Hence, I want to invite attention to this pervasive feature of the prayers in the book of Psalms.

What really got me thinking about and pursuing this dimension of the Psalms was a trip to Guatemala with a group of my students in 2001. More specifically, it was the opportunity to meet and listen to the testimony of a man named Jose Antonio Puac, who worked for several years during the 1990s for the Office of Human Rights of the Archdiocese of Guatemala, as this office produced a report called *Guatemala, Never Again! Recovery of Historical Memory Project.* The project was the equivalent to South Africa's Truth and Reconciliation process; it was an attempt to investigate, document, and tell the truth about the tens of thousands of persons killed, tortured, raped, and/or who disappeared in the civil strife in Guatemala between about 1960 and 1996.[3]

The report was presented publicly at the national cathedral in Guatemala City on April 24, 1998, by the Bishop of Guatemala City, Juan Gerardi, whom Jose Antonio Puac had served as right-hand man and to whom he had looked as mentor and friend. Two days later, Bishop Gerardi was brutally murdered in the garage of the rectory as he returned home. It was left to people like Jose Antonio to attempt to further publicize the report, which obviously was not well received by certain powerful people in high places in Guatemala. As our group sat in a room near the national cathedral in Guatemala City and listened to Jose Antonio as he told us about the report, about previous attempts on Gerardi's life, and about his concern for his own safety and that of his family, it struck me vividly and indeed viscerally—here is a man who knows that he has enemies! It really came home to me when Jose Antonio stood up during his presentation, walked over to the outside door to our room, and closed it cautiously. He explained, "There is a military office across the courtyard, and they might not like it if they know what I am telling you." At which point, of course, we all realized that we had enemies too, and we became a bit concerned for our own safety. We were fine, as it turned out; but I clearly remember thinking, and for the first time, even though I had been working intensively on the Psalms for many years: This must be what the psalmists actually felt like when they prayed the prayers for help in the book of Psalms!

As I have continued to think about Jose Antonio Puac and his courageous testimony and calling, another realization has struck me, especially as I consider my own life and experiences and those of other Christians in North American churches with whom I teach and learn about the Psalms—namely, we are *not* aware of having any enemies. In fact, when I am teaching the Psalms in churches, I regularly ask people whether they have any enemies; and almost without exception, the answer is *no*.

This presents, of course, a real difficulty in identifying with and appreciating the psalmic prayers, in which, as suggested above, the psalmists are *always* aware of having enemies. This difficulty is manifest often in peoples' honest response to a careful reading of the prayers for help in the book of Psalms—that is, people often conclude that the psalmists must have been "whiners" and that they just sort of needed to get a grip and pull themselves together. In other words, things could not have been as bad as the psalmists make them sound. In short, because we are not aware of having any enemies, we cannot imagine that they really did either. The most extreme example of this sort of response is one that I found in a book entitled *Diseases in Antiquity,* in which it was concluded that the psalmist's complaint about the enemies in Psalm 35 could be attributed to "schizophrenia simplex." It was further concluded that the psalmist's complaint about suffering in Psalm 38 represents "hypochondriacal ideas," and the complaints about the enemies in Psalm 38:12 represent "delusions" accompanying "a depressive psychosis."[4] In other words, the psalmists did not really have problems, and they did not really have enemies; rather, they were hypochondriacs and had paranoid delusions. But, as Jose Antonio Puac helped me to realize, it's not paranoia if they really are out to get you! Like the psalmists who claim to suffer and to have enemies on account of their faith, there are at least some Christians in the contemporary world who really do suffer and who really do have enemies, precisely as a result of their faith and what their faith leads them to say and do.

Now, the question that I pose for myself, as well as most other North American Christians who do not seem to be aware of having any enemies, is this: *Should* we have enemies? Without trying to be ambiguous or ambivalent, my answer is *yes* and *no*. No, we should not make it a goal to offend people or turn them against us. But yes, we probably should have enemies if we are faithful rather than simply innocuous. What Reinhold Niebuhr said seventy-five years or so ago is still on target: "[I]f a gospel is preached without opposition it is simply not the gospel which resulted in the cross. In short, it is not the gospel of love."[5] Let me be clear—the point is to be faithful, not offensive. In the same paragraph just quoted, Niebuhr also concludes: "An astute pedagogy and a desire to speak the truth in love may greatly decrease opposition to a minister's message and persuade a difficult minority to entertain at least, and perhaps profit by, his message."[6] Our calling is not to offend, but to proclaim the Word faithfully. If the Word, the gospel of love, is challenging, unsettling, and evokes opposition, as it always seems to, so be it.

So, from this perspective, maybe we should have enemies, as the psalmists *always* did. Of course, scores of books, monographs, and articles have been written in an attempt to identify the enemies in the Psalms, often from a cult-functional—that is, an essentially sociohistorical—perspective. For the purpose of preaching the Psalms, however, it seems more fruitful to proceed canonically. Who else in scripture is regularly opposed for attempting faithfully to proclaim and embody God's word and will for the world? The prophets, for one; and it is not coincidental that the book of Jeremiah contains several laments—often misleadingly labeled "Jeremiah's Confession"— in which he complains about the opposition that his faithfulness has evoked. And, of course, for Christians, it is Jesus, who from the beginning of his ministry is opposed and eventually crucified for preaching and embodying the gospel of love. As Marcus Borg aptly points out:

> Jesus, like the great social prophets of the Hebrew Bible, was a God-intoxicated voice of religious, social protest. He, like they, protested against and did a radical critique of the domination system of his day, just as they did of the domination systems of their day. Indeed, if one wants to ask the historical question, not "Why did Jesus

die?" but "Why was he killed?", the answer is, he was killed because of his passion for justice.[7]

Of course, it is not coincidental that the gospel-writers cannot tell the story of Jesus, especially the story of Jesus' passion and death, without frequent use of the Psalms, especially the prayers for help, in which, as we have seen, the psalmists are *always* opposed (see Pss. 22, 31, 41, 69, and 88).

These canonical connections, of course, press the question, If the faithful psalmists always had enemies, and if the prophets always had enemies, and if Jesus always had enemies, then why don't we? And at the same time, these canonical connections open up a fruitful possibility for understanding the enemies in the Psalms, a possibility that may even enable us to develop an awareness of whom or what *our* enemies should be. Taking as a clue the reality that the prophets and Jesus were opposed for faithfully proclaiming and embodying God's justice and love, one can proceed in the direction suggested by Roland E. Murphy: "[O]ne can see the 'enemies' [in the Psalms] as a symbol for the powers of evil arrayed against all that is good and just."[8] A virtually identical direction is articulated by James L. Mays:

> The enemies are out to deprive the afflicted of either shalom or *sedaqah* [usually translated "righteousness"—that is, the condition of things being right] or both. That is what makes them theologically important and what makes them a symbol that can be used in other and quite different social and cultural settings from the ones in which they were written...We pray because we desire that God's will and mind prevail—not our own, not others'.[9]

Note that both Murphy and Mays suggest that the enemies can be interpreted as "a symbol"; and as Mays suggests, this opens the way for appropriating in new "social and cultural settings" what the enemies symbolize. This includes *our* cultural setting. Note, too, that Mays mentions "God's will"; and both he and Murphy use terms that form an admirable summary of what God wills—good(ness), just(ice), righteousness, and shalom. When the Psalms portray the "coming" of the universal sovereign—that is, the presence of God in the world—they say that God is "coming" precisely "to establish justice (on) the earth. He will establish justice (in) the world with righteousness, and (among) the peoples with his faithfulness" (Ps. 96:13, author's trans.; see Ps. 98:9). Psalm 82 even suggests that the fundamental criterion for divinity is the will for and establishment of justice and righteousness (the root *shpt* occurs in 82:1, 2, 3, 8; and the root *sdq* occurs in 82:3); and quite congruently, the mission of the earthly king/messiah is put precisely in terms of justice and righteousness as well (Ps. 72:1–3), the result of which will be shalom, "peace" (Ps. 72:3, 7; NRSV "prosperity" in v. 3).

Hence, to pray and to preach the Psalms is to stand *for* God's will—goodness, justice, righteousness, and shalom—and to stand *against* the powers and forces that oppose God's will in the world. Thus, the Psalms, along with the prophets and Jesus, invite a spirituality or "ethic of resistance," to borrow a phrase from Douglas John Hall.[10] Our task as preachers involves identifying the powers and forces in our social and cultural setting that work in opposition to God's will for world-encompassing goodness, justice, righteousness, and shalom. And our task as preachers involves inviting people to stand *against* and resist such powers and forces—that is, to consider these powers and forces as our *enemies.*

What are the powers and forces in our social and cultural setting that oppose God's will for goodness, justice, righteousness, and shalom? They are legion, of course, and there are many directions that we might pursue in response to this question. But for illustrative purposes, as well as to provide some specificity, consider the following words of Martin Luther King Jr. They amount to a call to an "ethic of resistance," or as King puts it, a call to be "maladjusted":

> [T]here are some things in our social system to which all of us ought to be maladjusted...I never intend to adjust myself to the evils of segregation and the crippling effects of discrimination. I never intend to adjust myself to the inequalities of an economic system which takes necessities from the masses to give luxuries to the classes.

I never intend to become adjusted to the madness of militarism and the self-defeating method of physical violence. It may be that the salvation of the world lies in the hands of the maladjusted. The challenge to us is to be maladjusted.[11]

Given the state of race relations in the United States fifty years after *Brown* v. *Board of Education,* and given the current situation in Iraq, we might profitably and with good reason focus on what King calls the "evils of segregation" and "the madness of militarism," but I want to take us in the direction of a consideration of our "economic system," primarily because its debilitating and destructive effects are more subtle and less obvious.

One can make an exceedingly strong case that today, every bit as much as when King wrote the above words in 1958, our economic system is taking "necessities from the masses to give luxuries to the classes." It is still happening within the U.S., and perhaps the most visible example is that 44 million people in the U. S., including 8.5 million children, cannot afford, or in any case do not have, health insurance—a situation, by the way, that recently prompted a remarkable alliance between the National Council of Churches and the Southern Baptist Convention in support of Cover the Uninsured Week (May 10–16, 2004).

But the gap between rich and poor is even more dramatic beyond the U.S., and the phenomenon euphemistically known as "globalization" is not helping the situation. I say "euphemistically," because "globalization" sounds like something that the Psalms would be in favor of, given their proclamation of God as a universal sovereign who claims the whole creation as God's own (see Pss. 24, 93, 95–99, 148, 150). But the current form of globalization is not happening on God's terms. Rather, as 2001 Nobel Prize winner in economics, Joseph Stiglitz, points out, the kind of globalization that is taking place is a sort of economic imperialism on the part of the seven or eight richest nations on earth (the so-called G-7, or now with Russia, the G-8 nations); and the effect has been "to benefit the few at the expense of the many, the well-off at the expense of the poor."[12]

Particularly troubling to me is the way that the current form of globalization is driven by neo-liberal economic theory, which, as Stiglitz suggests by the language he uses to describe it, is something like a religion. As he puts it:

> The discontent with globalization arises not just from the economics seeming to be pushed over everything else, but because a particular view of economics—market *fundamentalism*—is pushed over all other views. Opposition to globalization in many parts of the world is not to globalization per se…but to the particular set of *doctrines*…that the international financial institutions [primarily the World Bank and the International Monetary Fund] have imposed…While many organizations would like to believe that they are indeed *infallible,* the problem with the IMF [International Monetary Fund] is that it often acts as if it *almost believes* in its own *infallibility*.[13]

Note the religious language—fundamentalism, doctrines, infallibility, belief. When the market-mechanism, or anything else, is viewed as essentially infallible, then the issue, in theological terms, is *idolatry*. No wonder that billions of people throughout the world are *discontent* with the current form of globalization!

In any case, for humanitarian reasons as well as for reasons related to economic theory, Stiglitz concludes that the current form of exclusively market-driven globalization must be opposed. In his words:

> If we are to address the legitimate concerns of those who have expressed a discontent with globalization, if we are to make globalization work for the billions of people for whom it has not, if we are to make globalization with a human face succeed, then our voices must be raised. We cannot, should not, stand idly by.[14]

Christians may be motivated to oppose the current form of globalization not only on humanitarian grounds, as Stiglitz does—that is, the fact that billions of impoverished people are discontent—but also on the grounds of our faith, including our reading, praying, and preaching of the Psalms. In Psalmic terms, insofar as the current form of globalization is a power "arrayed against" God's world-encompassing will for goodness, justice, righteousness, and shalom, *it is our enemy,* and it is to be opposed. In other words, to speak on behalf of those billions of impoverished, discontent people, and to advocate for what is good for them, rather than for what is good for the United States, will inevitably be an act of resistance.

To be sure, particular care is in order at this point, and Stiglitz gives us a clue that is helpful. The problem, he says, is not globalization per se, but rather the current form of it; and I would add that the problem is not capitalism per se, but rather the way that capitalism is often practiced without a human and humane face. In other words, the real problem, the real *enemy,* is greed.[15] Hence, we turn now to a further analysis of our enemy–greed–and its debilitating and destructive effects. The ultimate goal, however, will be to suggest that praise in the Psalms can serve as an antidote to the rampant greed that characterizes our everyday context.

Grace and Gratitude as a Cure for Infectious Greed: Praise in the Psalter

Taking as his point of departure the reality of the widespread impoverishment and discontent that Stiglitz highlights, Latin American theologian Victorio Araya offers the following assessment of both the contemporary world and contemporary theology:

> In view of the massive inequities in the contemporary world, we need a theology that affirms that life is an incredible gift of God for all people and all creation! Contemporary theology consists of asking what grace means today–that is, of asking what the good news means in a world that is full of bad news.[16]

We shall arrive at the good news in due course, but further consideration of the bad news is necessary as we continue to think about culture religiously and religion culturally. According to Federal Reserve chairman Alan Greenspan not too long ago, the bad news is that we in the United States are experiencing a national illness that he calls "infectious greed."[17] One would think, as a matter of common sense, that the more people have, the more content they would be and the more willing they would be to share out of their abundance. But it doesn't seem to work this way. Instead, it seems, the more people have, the more they want and the tighter they hold on to what they have. I am a Presbyterian, so let me cite us Presbyterians as a good example of a bad example, if you will. We Presbyterians are wealthy—not every one of us, of course, but on the average, we have the highest per-household income among all denominations in the U.S. Yet we average giving 2 percent of our income to the church, compared to Presbyterian giving of 3.3 percent in the 1930s.[18] This statistic represents greed in action; and it is rampant among us—indeed, it seems, a national illness, to which the church is not immune.

It's an embarrassment really. I have singled out Presbyterians, but the truth of the matter is that others are not doing all that much better than we are. The whole church stands to be embarrassed by our being infected with greed, which is why people such as Brian McLaren and others are trying to move the church toward what McLaren calls a "new kind of Christianity." In a recent book, McLaren imagines a running conversation between a traditionalist pastor and his friend, Neo (that is, "New"). McLaren's own vision of and for the church is obviously articulated by Neo, whose opinion at one point is being recalled by his pastor-friend, as follows:

> [Neo] said that if the new kind of Christianity we had been dreaming about wasn't radically generous, it was a waste of time. I responded by saying that it seemed like an overstatement to me, but he was adamant: "We live in the most affluent culture in the most affluent period of human history. If we can't discipline ourselves to learn the joys of generous living, I think we are an embarrassment to the gospel."[19]

Indeed! And this is precisely why pastors and teachers in the church simply have to be concerned with this national illness of "infectious greed," to which the church is not immune.

And of course, this illness, like other kinds of illness, presents a pastoral problem. "Infectious greed" has debilitating effects on individuals; because given the way that greed works, people are left perpetually wanting more, and hence constantly dissatisfied and oriented toward buying more stuff.[20] In fact, one of the symptoms of "infectious greed" is buying stuff that we don't need. According to clinical psychologist and *New York Times* best-selling author, Mary Pipher, we are experiencing a national crisis, which is essentially a crisis of meaning that results from our mistaken conclusion that buying more stuff will make us happy. In other words, the crisis involves "infectious greed," which, as Pipher points out, is driven in large part by advertising, which she calls our real "national religion."[21] We need not demonize advertisers, even though the name of the game in advertising is to create demand. But, of course, the advertisers could not so successfully create demand if you and I weren't so inclined already to pursue our happiness by buying more stuff. In any case, we consumers need to be very careful in the midst of an epidemic of greed, lest we simply pass on the infection by concluding that we never have enough and that we have to have more.[22]

The pastoral problem transcends the level of the individual, of course. On the corporate level, greed plays a major role in the kind of thing mentioned in the previous section—discontent among billions of impoverished people throughout the world. And within the U.S., there is not only the critical issue of health insurance and health care, but consider too the Enron and WorldCom debacles (which are probably the sort of thing that Chairman Greenspan had in mind when he made his diagnosis of "infectious greed"), as well as the deterioration of our national infrastructure, public schools that are constantly clamoring for adequate funding, and so on. As James M. Childs sums up the corporate effects of greed: "When greed is an integral part of the order of economic life and the rules of economic life become the arbiters of all relations and values in society, there is an inevitable neglect of the common good."[23] Then too, of course, as McLaren suggests, the church's being infected with greed proves to be an embarrassment to the gospel.

All of this is the bad news, but there is good news. There is a cure for "infectious greed," an antidote to the rampant greed that we live with everyday. In a word, it is gratitude, or what Mary Jo Leddy, in her book by this name, calls "radical gratitude."[24] And precisely at this point is where reading, praying, and preaching the Psalms becomes so crucially important, for the psalms of praise and thanksgiving commend to us "radical gratitude" over and over again.

The message is simple enough. Recall the words of Victorio Araya, with which this section began: "Life is an incredible gift of God for all people and all creation!" *Human life* is a gift! As Psalm 8:4–5 affirms:

> Then I ask, "Why do you care about us humans?
> Why are you concerned for us weaklings?"
> You made us a little lower than you yourself,
> and you have crowned us with glory and honor. (CEV)

The *life of all creation* is a gift! As Psalm 104:24 puts it:

> Our LORD, by your wisdom you made so many things;
> the whole earth is covered with your living creatures. (CEV)

The little and not-so-little things that sustain our lives, day by day, and year by year, are gifts! This is what the psalmists mean when they affirm, amid the pervasive presence of their enemies and amid constant turmoil and trouble, that God is their "refuge" (see Pss. 2:12; 5:11; 7:1; 16:1; and often, especially in Books I and II of the Psalter, where, as suggested in the previous section, the enemies are omnipresent).[25]

In a real sense, the fostering of radical gratitude in the Psalms comes down to the simple but deeply profound affirmation made in a verse such as Psalm 100:3: "It is God that made us, and we belong to God!" (my translation). Or a verse such as Psalm 24:1:

> The earth and everything on it belongs to the LORD.
> The world and its people belong to him. (CEV)

Think of that! We, and all those other billions of people out there, and even all of our stuff, belong to God! It is a message that begs to be proclaimed in our social and cultural setting of rampant, infectious greed!

Of course, it's a downright un-American message. We think that we *deserve* what we have; we have worked hard for it; we've earned it. But if we preachers and teachers in the church can get across the message of the Psalms–that we, and all of us, and all of our stuff, really belong to God–if we ourselves can manage to believe it and persuade others to believe it, the radical gratitude that would result from the experience of radical grace would be nothing short of astounding! I'll suggest just three possible and closely related results:

1. One result of *receiving* life as a gift rather than *achieving* it (or attempting to) would be that the unmitigated desire to acquire would be replaced by the desire to share. And think of what liberating contentment might follow, what genuine peace of mind and heart when we discover that it really is "more blessed to give"–that is, a source of greater happiness to give–"than to receive" (Acts 20:35).

2. This leads to a second and related result. It may be that we could be transformed from a society of greedy individualists, always looking out for ourselves and out for more, into a true society, characterized by responsive and responsible *solidarity*. From her reading of the letters of Paul, Elsa Tamez concludes that if life is understood as God's gift for all people and all creation–as the Psalms affirm, and as the affirmation of justification by grace in Paul's writing suggests–then no particular individual or group of people can claim to "deserve it" or to be superior to other individuals or groups. That is, the result of believing in grace will be the sort of radical gratitude that issues in solidarity.[26]

3. And a third and again related result of receiving life as a gift, of living by grace, of engaging in radical gratitude, would be, to return to Greenspan's diagnosis of our national illness, that we would become not a nation infected by greed, but rather we would become what we regularly say that we are–a nation of "liberty and justice *for all.*"

Contemporary philosopher James C. Edwards suggests that the paramount symbol for contemporary North American life is the shopping mall, because it lays out before us in one place the vast range of our consumer choices, including the actual stuff that we can buy in an attempt to define ourselves. It could be worse, Edwards thinks; but at the same time, he is afraid of the mall and to what happens to human identity when "shopping continues unabated"–things such as addiction, boredom, and what he calls "the triumph of the normal," a pervasive conformity that stifles any genuine creativity or newness. And oddly, since he is an avowed atheist, Edwards ends up arguing for the importance of "sacraments: deliberate occasions for a peculiar sort of grace…[that] would liberate unforeseen energies for change and modulate that change so as to control our tendency to limitlessly aggrandize the human."[27] In a thoroughly secularized way, then, Edwards is suggesting that there is a way to escape the trap of the mall and what it represents–that is, an "infectious greed" that threatens to yield addiction, boredom, and dangerous conformity. But what is so striking is that this thoughtful atheist cannot finally avoid the theological language of the Bible! The necessary cure for greed is grace! The way out of the mall's trap is the path of radical gratitude!

Edwards's analysis is extremely learned, interesting, and compelling; and his conclusions are urgently important–grace and gratitude are essential! But my guess is that the fostering of the affirmation that life is a *gift* will not happen by reading and expounding upon Plato and Descartes and Kierkegaard and Nietzsche, as Edwards does (although Kierkegaard may be helpful in this regard). To be sure, I am all in favor of reading and studying philosophy. But if grace is essential, then let's read and study and pray and preach the Psalms! To return to Victorio Araya's words, the Psalms regularly proclaim "that life is an incredible gift of God for all people and all creation!" The only appropriate response to this good news is to join the world-encompassing community of praise that the final verse of the Psalter invites us to join: "Let everything that breathes praise the LORD!" (Ps. 150:6). To join heaven and earth, to join all creatures and all creation in praising God is to engage in what Walter Brueggemann has aptly called "lyrical self-abandonment,"[28] which we might call the essence of radical gratitude and the ultimate in solidarity!

4

Preaching Community Laments

*Responding to Disillusionment with
God and Injustice in the World*

JOHN MARK HICKS

Communal lament seems different now, at least for Christians living in the United States. In the 1980s–1990s our national consciousness was triumphalist and optimistic. We were powerful. We won a ground war in 100 hours. We were wealthy. The economic greed of the 80s and the explosion of wealth in the 90s dominated our culture. We were both the world police and the world bank.[1]

But 9/11 changed our mood. Communal lament almost became the solution. Churches held special services. Television networks devoted time to remembrance. The entertainment industry empowered our lament. Lament brought the nation together. But in American culture communal lament quickly passes into private arenas as the materialistic, consumer-driven, and success-oriented spirit reemerges. American culture is unrelentingly optimistic, individualistic, and self-focused.

Communal lament, though sporadic in America's recent history, is embedded in the experience of many cultures. For example, the Ukrainian consciousness, given its history as victims of foreign oppression, is filled with and oriented toward lament. When I recently lectured on the Psalms in Kiev, the lament Psalms resonated with their experience more than the praise Psalms. The opposite is the case among suburban American churches.

Yet one subculture of the American experience is characterized by lament. The African American heritage is a culture of sorrow. While the church as a whole has picked up some of the "negro spirituals" that have nourished the African American church (e.g., "A Little Talk with Jesus," "He's Got the Whole World in His Hands," etc.), it has not generally embraced those that express lament in what W. E. B. Du Bois called the "sorrow songs." For example, these words would not fit well in most evangelical worship assemblies:

> Sometimes I feel like a motherless child
> Sometimes I feel like a motherless child
> Sometimes I feel like a motherless child
> A long ways from home
> There's praying everywhere.[2]

> Or:

> O Lord, O Lord
> Have mercy on me
> Trouble done bore me down
> O Lord, O Lord
> Have mercy on me
> Trouble done bore me down.
> I've seen some strangers quite unknown
> I'm a child of misery
> I'm sometimes up and sometimes down
> I'm sometimes level with the ground.
> O Lord, O Lord
> What shall I do,
> I asked God Almighty for to run me 'round
> O Lord, O Lord
> What shall I do?[3]

Such songs seem so distant to most suburban churches in America, even in our post–9/11 era. We are dominated by a liturgical style that is upbeat, perky, positive, and celebrative. We leave little room for songs that express the misery of life because, for the most part, we are communally disconnected from misery.

Yet these same suburban churches are filled with people who are disconnected from the churches' preaching and worship because it is so often triumphalist. Believers in the midst of lament find no voice and no community in churches where week in and week out the liturgy only expresses thanksgiving and joy. A mother who prayed intensely for months and endured bed rest for weeks only to suffer the birth of a stillborn enters a Sunday assembly the next week that is singing "God is so good." Her response is to weep alone in the women's restroom. A group of parents who have lost children feel distant from God partly because there is no sense of loss or hurt in their "church services," no manifestation of public lament in their community of faith. Because the community does not lament, lamenters sense that their faith is perceived as inauthentic; or worse, they think themselves faithless.

Yet Israel's experience was more similar to that of Ukrainians or African Americans than of American suburbia. Lament, or disorientation, characterizes almost half of the Psalms. Communal lament is definitely part of their communal expression of faith. Other than funerals and perhaps during Lent, American churches have few intentional and regular moments of communal lament. Preaching the communal laments of the Psalms is one way to recover that experience in the church.

Communal Laments in the Psalms

The narrative of Israel describes many occasions of communal lament. In fact, four of the seven situations envisioned in Solomon's dedicatory prayer for the temple in 2 Chronicles 6 are communal lamentations: defeat in battle (6:24–25), drought (6:26–27), natural disasters (6:28–31), and exile (36–39). In those moments the people come to the temple and pray. Jehoshaphat's prayer in the face of a Moabite invasion models what the chronicler described (2 Chr. 20:6–12).

These communal occasions followed some general patterns. The community engaged in a day of fasting,[4] perhaps including abstinence from sexual intercourse and normal activities (Joel 1:14; 2:15). They gathered before the Lord at the sanctuary.[5] The day might involve several different acts of mourning, including fasting,[6] wearing sackcloth and ashes,[7] and weeping.[8] Prayer was a central facet.[9]

The book of Psalms contains prayers that are communal in nature. They probably used moments of communal fasting, gathering, and prayer as described above. Like other cultures in the Ancient Near East, these communal lament Psalms were used not only on occasional days of mourning or anxiety, but also at regularly scheduled times in the Hebrew calendar. In other words, Israel had a liturgical cycle that included lament as well as praise and thanksgiving.[10]

Scholars have not reached a consensus in the identification of communal laments. Perhaps we are too technical in our identification of them, as all Psalms are ultimately placed in a communal liturgical context by their placement in the canon. They constitute Israel's liturgical handbook. But most scholars recognize the following Psalms as significant examples of a communal lament genre: 12, 14, 31, 35, 42–44, 53, 56, 58, 59, 60, 69, 74, 77, 79–80, 83, 85, 89, 90, 94, 102, 106, 108, 109, 123, 126, 129, 137, and 142.[11]

Though the structural components of communal laments are variously identified, Paul Wayne Ferris offers the most detailed picture:

1. *Invocation*–or direct address to God, calling God by God's name (Yahweh) or identifying a relationship with God ("my" or "our God").

2. *Hymn of Praise*–usually addresses God in the second person and recounts past acts.

3. *Expression of Confidence and Trust*–prior to the complaint: for example, that God is able and willing to hear; a trusting confidence that God is listening and will respond.

4. *Lament*–description of lamentable circumstances along with an expression of the anxiety, fear, and hurt that

accompanies those circumstances as well as the questions and doubts that arise within the believer.

5. *Appeal and Motivation for Response.*

   a. *for deliverance*–or redemption; seeks to move God to act on the ground of God's mercy, faithfulness, and/or love.

   b. *for cursing*–or imprecation; seeks to move God to avenge God's people on the ground of God's justice and righteousness.

6. *Protestation of Innocence*–rarely explicit, but the laments often reflect bewilderment and perplexity over the cause of their lamentable circumstance.

7. *Expression of Confidence and Hope*–expresses the expectation that God will deliver and act on behalf of God's people.

8. *Vow of Praise*–when the day of deliverance comes, they will praise God for God's redemptive act.[12]

Not all of the above components are found in every communal lament, and they are not necessarily in this order. But, according to Ferris, "invocation, the lament proper, and the appeal are the elements found in all communal laments."[13]

To illustrate the nature and function, as well as the preaching value, of communal lament Psalms, the next two sections will briefly survey Psalms 44 and 58.

Psalm 44 as Communal Disappointment with God

Israel had recently experienced defeat. Whether pre-exilic (e.g., 2 Chr. 14:9–10; 20:1) or exilic, a king or priest (cf. Pss. 44:4, 15–16) speaks for the people. Israel is bewildered by Yahweh's hostility and indifference despite their relative faithfulness. Their communal lament confronts God with complaint and accusation but at the same time appeals to God's faithful love. The Psalm moves from praise (1–3) and trust (4–8) through complaint (9–16) and protestation (17–22) to an ultimate appeal to God's loving faithfulness (23–26).[14] The center of the Psalm is a complaint directed at God's seeming unfaithfulness. The people were faithful, yet God was unfaithful. Nevertheless, though bewildered and angry, they invoke the faithful love of Yahweh.

The stories of God's mighty acts in Israel's history shape this poem as a background for communal lament. Israel's story as a corporate people shapes the individual lives of each person. Israel's story is their story and, more importantly, God's story. But the present stands in radical contrast (the adversative in verse 9–"but now" [NIV]) with God's past history with Israel. The series of second-person addresses in 9–14 presents God as the actor in the disaster that befell Israel. "The verbal presentation of God as taking drastic action *against* his people," Loren Crow observes, "is so surprising as to be doubly forceful. Its value is primarily shock."[15]

The protestations of innocence (17–18, 20–21) are each followed by an adversative ("yet") that describes God as the responsible party in their suffering (19, 22). The appeal is relational–it is an appeal to the relationship that the covenant formalizes and embodies. Israel feels betrayed. God has not been faithful to God's covenant. Though Israel boasts in God "all day long" (8, NIV), their disgrace is before them "all day long" (15) despite the fact that they have faced death for God's sake "all day long" (22). Israel is disappointed with Yahweh. The Shepherd watches his sheep being slaughtered (44:11, 22), and this creates the question, Where is God? (44:23–24).

The community appeals to their sleeping giant who is no longer pictured as the aggressor but as the inattentive Shepherd. The final appeal brings God's past salvific acts into the present as the motive or rationale for the petition. The appeal for redemption uses the language of the exodus (cf. Ex. 13:12; Deut. 13:6; Mic. 6:4; 1 Chr. 17:21). God's story is the norm by which God should act. God will eventually act out faithfulness to that norm which is God's faithful love. The petitions (23, 26) frame the questions (24–25). The petitions remind Israel of God's forever love for them, and this shapes the nature and function of their complaint. Israel complains in faith as it appeals to God's faithful love. God ultimately demonstrates that faithful love in Jesus Christ (Rom. 8:35–39).

Communal disaster evokes disillusionment and disappointment. It should also arouse introspection and self-examination as a communal process–sometimes in penitent confession, but sometimes (as in Psalm 44) with protestations of innocence.

Doubt, frustration, bewilderment, questioning, and complaint often arise in the hearts and prayers of the faithful people of God when they suffer.

Israel probably read Psalm 44 in times of national distress when they saw no seeming reason for the disasters that befell them as in the days of Asa or Jehoshaphat. Making a narrative of Psalm 44 in the life of Israel is a helpful way for us to contextualize it and create a link with our own narrative. Psalm 44 could have been proclaimed, sung, and prayed at the Mount Zion United Methodist Church in Philadelphia, Mississippi, during June 1964. On the seventeenth of that month, the African American church was burned, and on the twenty-first, seven members of the Ku Klux Klan murdered James Cheney, Andrew Goodman, and Michael Schwerner.

Psalm 44 could have been proclaimed, sung, and prayed by Christian churches in southern Sudan where the African Dinka people living in Bahr-El-Ghazal were raided in January 1996. Several of their daughters were taken into slavery.

Psalm 44 is even now proclaimed, sung, and prayed in memory of millions who died during the Nazi Holocaust, especially the six million Jews–a million of whom were children. The following is a contemporary midrash on Psalm 44:

> "You desert and shame us"–as they cut our beards and mass-rape our women.
>
> "You do not go out with our armies"–with our resistance.
>
> "You put us to flight from our enemies"–in mass exodus and transports.
>
> "Those who hate us tear us to pieces at will"–using our skins for lampshades and our flesh for soap.
>
> "You hand us over like sheep to be devoured"–in the gas chambers, crematoria, and gang burning-pits.
>
> "You cast us among the nations"–as stateless and displaced persons.
>
> "You sell Your people for nothing"–we are worth less than slaves, less than animals.

"You do not make a profit on their sale price"—our value is precisely calculated for work, starvation, and death.

"You make us an object of shame for our neighbors"—so that no one touches us, in the camps and even after liberation.

"A thing of scorn and derision for those around us"—they toss scraps of bread into the trains of our starving people; they make us defecate in our clothing.

"You make an example of us to the nations"—of degradation and dehumanization, a sign par excellence and a symbol of Jew-hatred.

"An object of head-shaking among the peoples"—in disbelief that something like this is happening to anyone, much less to us, Your chosen people.[16]

In the midst of communal tragedy, the people of God are bewildered by God's absence. We protest God's inaction or, more potently, God's violence against God's people, just as Israel did. However, Israel models for us that we should also remember God's past redemptive deeds and appeal to them. We remember God's faithful track record. Yet the present often seems so incongruent with that past. Why does God sleep? Why does not the Shepherd protect the sheep? Has God forgotten God's people? The present and the past do not line up. Something seems terribly wrong, even wrong with God. Nevertheless, the people of God maintain their covenant commitment as they appeal to God's faithful love. Given God's track record, the bewildered and confused community trusts even as it accuses.

The homiletic point is that in the midst of our distress we lament God's apparent hiddenness, but still we appeal to the unfailing love that characterizes God. Our God has a track record with God's people that reveals God's love, particularly the demonstration of that love in Jesus Christ.

Psalm 58 as Communal Zeal for Justice

Occasioned by the injustices of the ruling class, the community petitions God to judge their unjust judges. A worshiper speaks for the community in a kind of "cultic prophetic lament."[17] The lamenter complains about unjust leaders and their wickedness (1–5), petitions for their removal (6–9), and praises God for God's justice in advance (10–11). When human leaders fail to administer justice in the world, the God who judges the earth will judge them; and the people of God appeal for divine action against unjust judges. The imprecatory petition of verse 6 is the structural center of the lament, framed by the verb "judge" in verses 1 and 11. Human judges, who sit in God's judgment seat, act out of self-interest rather than for the sake of the kingdom of God. They deserve God's curse. Consequently, Israel complains about injustice, appeals for justice, and expects God's righteous judgment.

The judges ("gods") do not act according to covenantal equity. Instead, they devise inequities in their hearts and carry out their design with violence. They are like cobras with their lies–they destroy; they intend to do evil. They are like deaf cobras in that no one can charm them–they are incorrigible. As James Mays comments, "They are so enchanted with the lie of their life that they are deaf and blind to any other influence."[18] The psalmist calls on God to act–to defang the judges or take away their power. Unjust judges deserve to wither rather than blossom. Thus, the lamenter seeks their demise according to the figures (drain, wither, dissolve, miscarry) of verses 7–9. Here, the joy of the righteous is rooted in a just God's defeat of the wicked.

The reality of a victimized world must be taken seriously, especially when structures of power oppress the poor. The lament evokes a vision of God's justice that takes the side of the oppressed over against those who abuse their power. It challenges us to enter into their experience and cry to the Lord with them. It challenges us to seek God's kingdom and God's righteousness. "The words which we have sung," Augustine preaches, "must be rather hearkened to by us, than proclaimed. For to all men as it were in an assemblage of mankind, the Truth crieth, 'If truly indeed justice ye speak, judge right things, ye sons of men.'"[19] Consequently, Erich Zengar appropriately comments, "The psalm fights for the indispensable union of religion and ethics. The truth about God that people believe or proclaim can be tested by whether it preserves its adherents from the ways of violence and impels them to a life in solidarity with the victims of violence."[20]

This psalm expresses righteous indignation against structural injustice within society. It laments the wickedness that pervades human social institutions. It offers a form by which oppressed people may pray for God's justice in their land.

Israel's struggle with injustice continues as our struggle. Just as this Psalm arose out of the narrative of Israel's oppression by its own leaders (cf. Jer. 22), so our proclamation of this Psalm must be placed in our history. Dietrich Bonhoeffer preached this Psalm only days after key church leaders, including Martin Niemöller, were arrested on July 1, 1937. Bonhoeffer railed against the injustice that was sweeping his country and called on God to act.[21] We can hear the cries of African American churches during the civil rights movement of the 1960s. We can hear the cries of Palestinian mothers whose homes are blown up by Israelis because the sons were involved in illegal activities.[22]

If we proclaim Psalm 58, however, it will make demands on us. It will call us to stand with the oppressed and empathize with the victims of injustice. But as we share the experience of the marginalized, oppressed, and poor, the Psalm calls us to leave vengeance in the hands of God. It is God's work, not ours. Bonhoeffer made this clear for his own church under Nazi oppression:

> It would mean much if we would learn that we must earnestly pray to God in such distress and that whoever entrusts revenge to God dismisses any thought of ever taking revenge himself. Whoever does take revenge himself still does not know whom he is up against and still wants to take charge of the cause by himself. But whoever leaves revenge in God's hands alone has become willing to suffer and bear it patiently-without vengeance, without a thought of one's own revenge, without hate, and without protest; such a person is meek, peaceable, and loves his enemies. God's cause has become more important to him than his own

sufferings. He knows God will win the victory in the end. "Vengeance is mine, says the Lord, I will retaliate" (Deut. 32:35)–and he will retaliate. But we are free from vengeance and retribution. Only the person who is totally free of his own desire for revenge and free of hate and who is sure not to use his prayers to satisfy his own lust for revenge-only such a person can pray with a pure heart: "Shatter the fangs of the young lions, O Lord, break the teeth in their mouth."[23]

Even more dangerously, however, is how Psalm 58 calls us to reassess our own relationship with the oppressed and victimized. Are we certain that we do not participate in the structural realities that oppress the poor and victimize the marginalized? As we proclaim this Psalm, we must confront our own life. Zengar offers an important perspective:

> In the process, they very often compel us to confess that *we ourselves* are violent, and belong among the *perpetrators* of the violence lamented in these psalms. *In that way,* these psalms are God's revelation, because in them, in a certain sense, God in person confronts us with the fact that there are situations of suffering in this world of ours in which such psalms are the last things left to suffering human beings–as protest, accusation, and cry for help. It is obvious on the face of it that these psalms are contextually legitimate on the lips of victims, but a blasphemy in the mouths of the executioners, except as an expression of willingness to submit oneself, with these psalms, to God's judgment.[24]

The cry for justice against injustice is not unchristian. On the contrary, we cry out for justice (vengeance) as we await the coming Son of Man (Lk. 18:7–8). The parable of the persistent widow is particularly appropriate for the proclamation of Psalm 58, as a widow cries out for justice against an unjust judge.[25] Further, should we not rejoice in the day of justice (vengeance) when God's kingdom is fully established (Rev. 19:1–4)? Did not the saints under the altar pray for such a day (Rev. 6:10; cf. 18:20). Christologically, the Son will execute vengeance upon the unjust (2 Thess. 1:8), and believers will find rest in that justice. The Thessalonian epistle addresses young, persecuted Christians who find hope in the eschatological vengeance of the second coming of Christ. Preaching imprecatory Psalms needs both an eschatological perspective and a sense of the present in-breaking of the kingdom of God that establishes justice and righteousness in the earth.[26]

Homiletically, when we find empathy with the oppressed, we must stand in their place and pray for the revelation of God's justice. Psalm 58 not only cries out for justice, it invites hearers to stand with the oppressed and act on their behalf.

Communal Laments and Worship

In many ways the contemporary church is recovering the value of lament in private prayer. The recovery of individual lament Psalms in the life of believers is growing, is encouraged by many, and easily connects with the experience of the psalmists. That was my own entrance into the world of the Psalms, as it has been for many.[27] But Walter Brueggemann warned us twenty years ago that while the "recovery of personal lament is a great gain," if the communal laments are not "set along side, the record of personal religion can serve only privatistic concerns—and that is no doubt a betrayal of biblical faith."[28] Without faithful communal lament, the church continues the dominant privatization of faith and fails to "think *theologically* about public issues and public problems."[29]

Without faithful communal lament, private hurts live in tension with public joy. Those who regularly attend celebrative and even contemplative liturgical assemblies sense that they are inauthentic Christians or that those assemblies are inauthentic because they do not connect with their experience of lament and suffering. Although they may bring their hurts and pains to support groups, to small groups, or even to their pastors in private, they have no access to the communal or shared expression of lament in their liturgies. Ultimately, their community does not weep with them but projects a joy that they do not experience. Consequently, when they attend those joyous assemblies without the opportunity of lament or the encouragement to lament, they feel like outsiders rather than participants, like hypocrites rather than authentic people, because their joy is forced rather than experienced.

Without faithful communal lament, the cry for social justice remains behind the closed doors of private discussions. Or worse, it is left in the hands of faithless secular advocates, and the community of faith has no voice in the public square. Without communal lament, social justice becomes the task of the individual rather than the church.

Without faithful communal lament, sin and injustice remain private matters of individualistic concern. Sin and injustice, just as spirituality itself, remain private. It is an individual problem and not a structural one. It is a personal problem and not a generational one.

Without faithful communal lament, communities of faith do not share the hurt and pain of public, national, or global tragedies and anxieties. Without faithful communal lament, we do not participate as communities in the realities of the human predicament. Consequently, we exist as superficial, inauthentic, and uncaring communities in a fallen world filled with hurts and pains.

Unfortunately, communal lament is often perceived as a "downer." Boomers have often told me that they do not want lament in their worship time because they come to "church" to be revived and not to be brought down. Boomer worship renewal has often meant emphasizing the joy of celebrative worship to the exclusion of lament. One problem with this statement is a misunderstanding of lament. Lament for the lamenter is not a "downer," but a necessary expression of faith. It sustains hope. Yet if we use communal laments as a means to wallow in the sorrow of the human predicament so that it amounts to no more than self-pity, then we misunderstand the function of lament. Lament transforms. Lament enables perseverance. Lament empowers. Lament gives hope, because embedded in the lament is an appeal that arises out of trust in the God whose love is forever. Lament is the mode by which hope is reborn.[30]

W. E. B. Du Bois, the turn-of-the-century African American author who voiced the hopes and dreams of African American people, called the "slave songs" of his people their "sorrow songs." But, he argued, the songs embodied hope:

> Through all the sorrow of the Sorrow Songs there breathes a hope—a faith in the ultimate justice of things. The minor cadences of despair change often to triumph and calm confidence. Sometimes it is faith in life, sometimes a faith in death, sometimes assurance of boundless justice in some fair world beyond. But whichever it is, the meaning is always clear: that sometime, somewhere, men will judge men by their souls and not by their skins.[31]

Lament is an act of faith. It is an appeal to divine faithfulness. Consequently, it assumes hope or at least will yield hope.

Perhaps we do not have communal laments for another reason. Perhaps our liturgies are not about community in the first place. Perhaps our liturgies are about the self, the individual. Perhaps we lack an authentic sense of weeping with those who weep.

Can our assemblies become a place of weeping as well as celebrating? Can our triumphalist concept of worship make room for lament in our liturgy? Biblical faith demands that it must. Half of the Psalms give voice to disorientation, hurt, and pain. Half of Israel's public liturgy was lament. Communal lament must become part of our church life. If we are to share the story of Israel and its life of faith, lament must become part of our liturgy.

Conclusion

In the wake of 9/11 the church has learned the value of communal lament.[32] It is a lesson we learned, but perhaps it had only a momentary impact. The first anniversary was observed by many; but the second lost ground, and the third anniversary lost even more. My point is not that we should institute an annual liturgical memorial day for 9/11, though I would not oppose such a move. Rather, my point is that communal lament, though it had a brief brilliant life, has not become part of the regular cycle of our liturgical experience.

Communal lament needs to become, as it was for Israel, part of the rhythm of our liturgical life.[33] It is part of the rhythm of our human experience; consequently, it should become part of our divine service. We need communal moments of penitence (e.g., Lent). We need communal moments of memorial for past or present national tragedies (e.g., 9/11). We need communal moments of prayer for justice in the world and our society (e.g., Martin Luther King Day). We need communal moments of memory for those who died in our congregations (e.g., an annual day of remembrance).

Preaching communal laments, however, will not only give voice to the cry of the disoriented but will also become a word of God to the disoriented. Through the communal lament the church expresses its lament, hurt, and pain; but also through hearing the communal lament of Israel's past it hears a word of God that gives hope in the present. The Word bears witness to God's faithfulness and rehearses Israel's own memory of God's mighty acts.

The "sorrow songs" of African American liturgy enabled an oppressed community to endure through faith. The 9/11 remembrance services express our continued pain and hurt but also call us to peace and justice. Lament services as part of the cycle of our Sunday morning rhythm will empower and transform the hurting as the church weeps with those who weep. The present is a good moment for the renewal of communal lament in our churches through the preaching of communal laments.

5

The New Testament Preaches the Psalms

Problems and Possibilities

RONALD COX

The Psalms have been very good to modern critical scholarship. From Hermann Gunkel to Walter Brueggemann, scholarly study of the Psalms has yielded a hundredfold. It certainly has increased our appreciation for the literary and historical nature of the Psalter and of scripture in general. As significant, if not more so, is the fact that critical scholarship of the Psalms has proven so beneficial for their spiritual appropriation. The identification of and investigation into the lament form in particular is an invaluable boon to pastoral ministry. Graduate seminars on the Psalms have been known to impact how ministers approach hospital visits, funerals, and a host of pastoral duties.

At the same time, perhaps nothing serves better to highlight the *differences* between the way ancients read scripture and the way we read it today than contemporary Psalms scholarship. Ancient students of the Psalms did not ask of the Psalms the questions we have been trained to ask, questions relating to whether a psalm is a lament or praise, personal or communal, a song of Zion or of the exile, a psalm of disorientation or of reorientation, and so on. By all of these, we have this strong desire to know and make connection with the historical situation of the psalmist; our forbearers in the interpretation process (from even before the NT [New Testament]) appear to have been more concerned with their own historical situation.[1] And so their exegesis of the Psalms often appears to be an exercise in getting from the biblical word(s) to their own *Sitz im Leben* in the quickest route possible.

This is quite problematic for us as Christians because the NT is authoritative for us.[2] No matter how tempted we may be to say "Paul knew Hillel, but I know Westermann and Mowinckel," Paul's reading of the Psalms still trumps ours in the perspective of the great cloud of witnesses that is the church. Rather than be cowed by tradition or repudiate it, we must, of course, learn to dialogue with it (even if in the end–as I believe–we must always be prepared to say "Yes, ma'am," and do as we are told).

This chapter is an exercise in such dialogue. Here, I wish to bring together the way the Psalms are read by NT authors and the way we read them today and to consider what may come of it. First, I will describe the general perspective on the Psalms that the NT shares with other turn-of-the-era interpreters, especially those at Qumran. This will allow us to identify the key differences that prove most problematic. Next, I will consider instances where we may profitably correlate the NT reading of the Psalms with our own. The space allowed permits only a sampling of possibilities. I have chosen three I consider most suggestive: the reading of Psalm 95:7b-11 in Hebrews 3:7–4:11; the reading of Psalm 2:1–2 in Acts 4:23–31; and the reading of Psalm 22 in Mark 15.

The Problem of the Pesher[3]

We turn now to a sect that broke away from mainstream Judaism to rally around its founder, a teacher at odds with the Jerusalem establishment and–from the perspective of his followers–persecuted by that establishment. The sect identified itself as the legitimate continuation of the faith of Israel and was at odds to show how its practices, beliefs, and interpretation of Israelite scriptures were more in keeping with the will of God than those of the majority of the Jews.

Among the biblical texts this sect could turn to, the Psalms were what they most relied upon. While they clearly used the Psalms in their worship, they appear to have considered them equally valuable as prophetic texts. Biblical prophecy in general was very important to the sect, as it was the primary means by which they sought to demonstrate their status as *the* people of Israel. They read the prophecy as speaking about their current time and in particular believed the prophecy was about the opposition and ultimate vindication of the Teacher, who was their leader. Hence, viewing the Psalms as prophecy, they read them as speaking about this Teacher of theirs and about his struggle with the Jewish establishment. The sect, of course, is Christianity, and all of this is why I think we find the NT use of the Psalms so distinctive from our own historically-oriented approach.

On the other hand, all these characteristics were not unique to the early Christians. The same features characterize the community that generated the Dead Sea Scrolls. Though the details and outcome are very different, the general story of the Essenes at Qumran is still quite *similar* to that of the early Christians.[4] They were a sect that recoiled against the ruling Jewish establishment and rallied around a disenfranchised leader, the Teacher of Righteousness. In their monastery near the Dead Sea they practiced religion as they believed it should be, focusing on an alternative calendar and radical purity rituals, all of which set them off from the Jewish majority.

Most important for our purposes is their approach to scripture. As the greatest number of citations in the NT are from the Psalms, so also the greatest number of scripture fragments at Qumran are from the Psalms (followed again by Deuteronomy and Isaiah).[5] The Psalms clearly were part of the Qumran liturgy, though they also held the status of prophetic texts.[6] Again, the Dead Sea Essenes interpreted biblical prophecy (including the Psalms) in terms of their own time (the rise of the Hasmonean kingdom) and especially in terms of their leader, the Teacher of Righteousness (possibly a priest who lost out in a Jerusalem power struggle).

Much can be made, and much has been made, of the affinities between the Qumran literature and the NT. In this study, I only want to highlight a few things. First, if we may take both movements as representative of the time, we are struck by the value ancient Judaism placed on the Psalms.[7] However they were used, for liturgy or as prophecy, the Psalms appear to have a power and a resonance that allowed them to endure well beyond the temple setting. I am inclined to think that their preservation and their being so highly regarded is indebted to the attribution of the Psalms to David. Davidic authorship tied to the hope of the restoration of the kingdom of Israel make the Psalms visionary texts about a reconstituted relationship with God and the world.

It is beneficial to know the interrelationship between the prophetic reading of the Psalms and their liturgical use. How does one sing a psalm that one interprets as referring to the Teacher of Righteousness? Although we know that the Psalms were used liturgically (cf. Eph. 5:19//Col 3:16), we have little evidence as to how they were used. Furthermore, Davidic attribution causes a bewildering bifurcation with respect to the function of the Psalms. The Psalms retain their liturgical quality, yet once associated with David they become historical in orientation.[8] Yet a historical orientation had a different connotation at Qumran and in the NT than what it does today. History is not simply about events and persons in the past but about how those events and people anticipate the contemporary situation of the Essenes or of Jesus and his followers. For them, history was a forward-looking, eschatological concept. Hence, David's authorship becomes the basis for reading the psalms as prophecy. We read in the Qumran Psalms Scroll:

> And David, son of Jesse, was wise, and a light like the light of the sun, and learned, and discerning, and perfect in all his paths before God and men. And YHWH gave him a discerning and enlightened spirit. And he wrote

psalms…and songs…The total was four thousand and fifty. All these he spoke through (the spirit of) prophecy which had been given to him from before the Most High.[9]

In the New Testament, David's inspiration is more succinctly stated, often prefacing a psalm by saying the Spirit speaks "through David" or "David by the Spirit says."[10] It may be as simple as "David says" followed by a prophetic reading of a psalm (e.g., Lk. 20:42; Acts 2:25; Rom. 11:9).[11] All of this leads to the sense that the greatness of David's Psalms has little to do with his status as king or his life experience; he is the reliable prophet who serves as a conduit for God's Word.

Whereas this may have invested the Psalms with greater utility and preserved their place in the community's life and worship, the prophetic understanding produces an approach to the Psalms that causes the modern Psalms reader much consternation. We are trained to read a psalm (or even a group of psalms) as a complete text, to observe its various features, to consider its rhetorical moves, and to contemplate what its original setting may have been. The reading the Essenes and early Christians practiced would seem to thwart our efforts at every turn.

First, their approach focused on psalm fragments rather than on complete psalms. In the NT it is very rare to find portions of psalms cited that are longer than one or two lines.[12] Consider Psalm 110:1: "The LORD says to my Lord, 'Sit at my right hand until I make your enemies your footstool.'" This line occurs in several places in the NT, always with reference to Jesus. "Sitting at God's right hand" becomes code for Jesus' ascension to the Father after his resurrection.[13] Both the psalm and its interpretation have to do with enthronement, but the context of the verse is never mentioned.[14] The first verse stands alone and does not need the remaining verses.

At first glance, the Dead Sea Scrolls appear to offer a counter example, namely, the Pesherim on Psalm 37.[15] Psalm 37 is an acrostic Wisdom psalm describing the fates of the righteous and the wicked. The Qumran interpretation makes much of these delineations, seeing the righteous as the Teacher and his followers, the wicked as the Jewish establishment at Jerusalem.

However, closer inspection shows that each pesher is separate from the next. Apart from the contemporary context to which the psalms are applied, no overriding logic or literary concern arising from the psalm unifies the pesherim on Psalm 37.

The pesherim on Psalm 37 reveal another source of consternation. The psalm's *Sitz im Leben* is ignored.[16] The pesherim show no concern for what situation Psalm 37 originally addressed, who the righteous and wicked are in a Sapiential context; all that matters is the *commentator's* context. Another example of this is Psalm 45, the original *Sitz im Leben* of which was clearly a wedding of an Israelite king. Disregarding this, Hebrews 1:8–9 apply Psalm 45:6–8 (which begins "Your throne O God, endures forever" and includes the phrase "God, your God, has anointed you") to Jesus. Interestingly, the Pesherim on Psalm 37 in the Dead Sea Scrolls are followed immediately by fragments of pesherim on Psalm 45. The last fragment includes part of an interpretation of verse 2 ("[M]y tongue is like the pen of a ready scribe") that is applied to the Teacher of Righteousness.[17]

Finally, in addition to a fragmented reading of the Psalms and a discounting of their original setting, the prophetic approach views each psalm as having the same form. When it came to Psalm 37, the Qumran exegete saw only an inspired mystery to be worked, not an acrostic poem or a Wisdom psalm. The writer to Hebrews knows Psalm 45:6–8 not as a royal psalm, but as the source of one in a series of proof texts he uses for highlighting the dignity of the Son. Clearly, the use of Psalm 110:1 to refer to Jesus' ascension corresponds to the enthrone-ment of the king about which the psalm originally spoke. However, this is most likely a secondary, perhaps even an accidental development. If we may take Jesus' use of Psalm 110:1 in the gospels (Mt. 22:43–45; Mk. 12:36–37; Lk. 20:42–44) as reflective of its earliest interpretation, we see that it stood out more for its puzzling reference by *David* to someone, not himself and not God, as Lord ("The LORD said to my Lord…").

What are we to do with the NT's approach to the Psalms? After all, this is the tradition we have inherited, the canon we place ourselves under as Christian preachers and teachers. Yet I do not know of an Old Testament professor who would approve of our adopting the NT approach to the Psalms with its apparent disregard for the form, setting, and literary structure of the Psalter.

In terms of a formulating a response, I first would suggest that the strong similarities between NT exegesis of the Psalms and that of the Qumran Scrolls should be viewed as a positive. From this comparison we can see that the NT is a product of its time and that its prophetic approach to the Psalms is not, strictly speaking, divinely ordained (unless we want to rethink our stands concerning solar calendars and ritual purification and other activities Essene). Hence, we can rest somewhat easier knowing we share with the NT more than its *kerygma*. Also, like it, we are products of our time. It seems to me that knowing these things about the NT and about ourselves allows us to consider its use of the Psalms in a constructive fashion, allowing both the NT and the Psalms to speak.

"Today, If You Hear His Voice…"
Psalm 95:7a-11 in Hebrews 3:6—4:11

Lest we conclude that the NT reading of the Psalms as eschatological prophecy lacks subtlety, we begin by examining the use of Psalm 95 in the anonymous epistle to the Hebrews. Following a comparison of Jesus and Moses in Hebrews 3:1–6, both of whom were faithful to God, the author of Hebrews moves to a call for faithfulness on the part of his audience: "Take care, brothers and sisters, that none of you may have an evil, unbelieving heart that turns away from the living God" (3:12). The call finds its force in a negative example, the Israelites of the exodus generation who rebelled against God in the wilderness for testing at Massah and quarreling at Meribah (Ex. 17:1–7). The example is brought forward by means of Psalm 95:7b-11, quoted in Hebrews 3:7–11.

> Therefore, as the Holy Spirit says, "Today, if you hear his voice, do not harden your hearts as in the rebellion, as on the day of testing in the wilderness, where your ancestors put me to the test, though they had seen my works for forty years. Therefore I was angry with that

generation, and I said, 'They always go astray in their hearts, and they have not known my ways.' As in my anger I swore, 'They will not enter my rest.'"[18]

Psalm 95 itself is one in series of enthronement psalms, all of which form what may be the "heart of the psalter," a recognition of YHWH as Israel's true king and an affirmation of his rule.[19] Psalm 95 begins with a call to worship YHWH on the basis of his being "a great God, and a great King above all gods" whose possession is the world "which his hands have formed" (vv. 1–5). Verses 6–7a restate the call to worship YHWH, but for a less global, more personal reason: YHWH is "our Maker" and "our God, and we are the people of his pasture, and the sheep of his hand." To this point, the psalm has made a subtle yet powerful comparison between the Lord's cosmic rule and his rule of his people: He is the maker of both, holding both in his hand. The emphasis is clear, "The 'great God' (v. 3) is 'our God' (v. 7a)";[20] what God is for the world God is specifically and personally for Israel ("*our* God," "*our* Maker," "*our* shepherd"; they are the people of "*his* pasture, the sheep of *his* hand"). The "great God" had made a covenant relationship with a specific people, Israel.

There is a clear shift at Ps. 95:7b: "O that today you would listen to his voice!" This is a transitional line that calls the listener's attention to the present ("today") need to "listen" to God.[21] What follows in 95:8–11 appears to be spoken "in God's voice," possibly in the form of an oracle given by a temple representative.[22] The essence of this oracle is a demand by God, "Do not harden your hearts," backed by a warning: God might again be brought to anger as he was when the Israelites tested him in the wilderness after the exodus. The psalm concludes with God's decision back at Meribah and Massah, "They shall not enter my rest," which also serves as an ominous if indirect threat to the psalm's intended audience. There is no return to praise or other positive note to end the psalm (contrast Ps. 81:12–16).

Turning back to Hebrews, the author does not appear to be in any way concerned with the cosmic or national claims of Ps. 95:1–7a. Instead, he moves directly to the negative example. This is not surprising, as the Hebrews' author has a tendency to be rather stern with his audience, speaking frankly with them about the consequences of faithlessness and disobedience (cf. Heb. 5:11–6:8; 10:31; 12:15–17).[23] The whole passage (Ps. 95:7b–11) is important to his argument, but he specifically emphasizes two lines: verses 7b–8a, "Today, if you hear his voice, do not harden your hearts"; and v. 11, "As in my anger I swore, 'They will not enter my rest.'" From these the author focuses on three concepts: the consequences of an unbelieving (or "hardened") heart; a reworking of the meaning of "rest"; and an encouragement to enter that rest "today" by means of faithfulness. His argumentation is complex, as it does not progress point by point but moves about in something of a circular fashion. However, the author's purpose is clear: He is applying the psalmist's warning "in a new and imaginative way to his own congregation."[24]

In terms of the consequences of an unbelieving heart, we have already seen that the use of the negative example of the rebellious Israelites in the wilderness is straightforward and consistent with the psalm's own use. The Hebrews author expounds on these lines of the psalm in 3:16–19 to make it perfectly clear that those who fell because of sin were the very same whom God brought out of Egypt, yet this did not stop them from suffering God's wrath due to their unbelief. The clarity comes when the author throws in an image from Numbers 14:29: God was angry with "those who sinned, whose bodies fell in the wilderness" (Heb. 3:17). Thus does the author intensify an already intense passage.

To make the case that the psalm's message is still efficacious, the Hebrews author demonstrates a surprising historical sensitivity, surprising, that is, given the typical manner of reading the Psalms prevalent during his time.[25] He desires to demonstrate that the "the promise of entering [God's] rest is still open" even if the majority of the exodus generation missed out. He does this by rescribing the meaning of "rest" so that it refers not to the occupation of Canaan but to something else altogether. The argument is worth quoting in its entirety.

> For we who have believed enter that rest, just as God has said, "As in my anger I swore, 'They shall not enter my rest,'" though his works were finished at the foundation

of the world. For in one place it speaks about the seventh day as follows, "And God rested on the seventh day from all his works." And again in this place it says, "They shall not enter my rest." Since therefore it remains open for some to enter it, and those who formerly received the good news failed to enter because of disobedience, again he sets a certain day–"today"– saying through David much later, in the words already quoted, "Today, if you hear his voice do not harden your hearts." For if Joshua had given them rest, God would not speak later about another day. (Heb. 4:3–8)

This passage is a rich example of early Jewish scriptural exegesis and has a number of attributes worth considering. Let me just concentrate on two. The author employs a standard exegetical argument of the time when he (re)interprets the term *rest* in Psalm 95:11 ("they shall not enter my *rest*") by linking it with the same term in Genesis 2:2 ("God *rested* on the seventh day").[26] In doing this, he makes clear that for him the Sabbath rest is not just limited to creation but is also an eschatological concept ("a sabbath rest still remains," Heb. 4:9).[27] By this simple verbal link the author renders Psalm 95 an eschatological prophecy. He backs this up with a reference to David (v. 7), to whom the LXX attributes the psalm.[28] David's historicity is valued here along with his status as inspired prophet. Because he clearly comes generations after Joshua, when David as the psalmist speaks ("much later") of the prospect of entering God's rest "today," he must be referring to another day and anther rest than that provided by Joshua, that is, the land.

Even if we did not share the author's eschatological perspective, we must admit he has a point. Psalm 95 clearly represents an effort to bring the experience of the exodus generation to bear on a later people at a later time. Because the weight of the oracle comes in its semi-veiled threat of not entering God's rest (95:11), that rest must refer to something other than what the exodus generation hoped for. Furthermore, it is natural and no small part of the author's argument to focus on the "today" of the psalm as an eschatological day. His treatise begins by noting how "in these last days [God] has spoken to us by a Son" (Heb. 1:2). Later, he will exhort his audience to continue to encourage one another "and all the more as you see the Day approaching" (10:25).[29] The author must have intended for his audience to see the clock ticking with respect to their decision to remain faithful. One moment he powerfully depicts to his audience the nature and work of the Son; the next moment he verbally cajoles them for their lack of faith. All the while he notes that they only have "today" to respond.[30]

Finally, the rhetorical force of the argument in both the psalm and in Hebrews is divine attribution. The phrase "O that today you would listen to [God's] voice" sets up the oracle to come. The Hebrews author views verse 7b along with verses 8–11 of Psalm 95 as having prophetic status: "as the Holy Spirit says" (Heb. 3:7). Still, we should not discount the importance of Psalm 95:7b to the author. References to God's speaking form an inclusion that brackets the argument of Hebrews (1:1–2, 12:25–29), and it is clear throughout the "epistle" that the author views the divine speech act as having salvific significance. The divine speech that concludes Psalm 95 is but one among a myriad of instances ("in many and various ways," Heb. 1:1) in which God speaks for human benefit. Although the Christ event may be the ultimate expression of God (1:2), the author understands God's Word to have an enduring consistency and efficacy that shapes and inspires even his own "word of exhortation" (13:22). Caught up in the power of God's voice to speak from a psalm of David to his audience's need, he steps back from his argument to confess:

> Indeed, the word of God is living and active, sharper than any two-edged sword, piercing until it divides soul from spirit, joints from marrow; it is able to judge the thoughts and intentions of the heart. And before him no creature is hidden, but all are naked and laid bare to the eyes of the one to whom we must render an account. (Heb. 4:12–13)

This confession is telling. We learn from it something of what it means that God speaks to us in the Psalms. The Hebrews author does not–indeed, he cannot–domesticate the prophetic voice of Psalm 95:7b-11. The historical critic might choose to designate this oracle a relic of ancient history. The eschatological zealot might enslave it to the minutia of his own context. But our author simply stands in awe of the psalm. He dares to read it as God's living voice still speaking, today, to him and through him to his audience with façade-destroying bluntness and soul-piercing relevance. He dares to do this. The question is: Do we?

"Why Do the Nations Conspire, and the Peoples Plot in Vain?"

Psalm 2:1–2 in Acts 4:23–32

According to Acts 3:1–4:22, sometime after Pentecost, Peter and John encounter a lame man outside the temple. Peter works a miracle, healing that man in the name of Jesus. A crowd gathers and Peter and John proclaim to them the word about Jesus and his resurrection, only to be arrested by the temple authorities and eventually made to stand trial before the Jerusalem rulers (Acts 4:5–6). After the apostles make a bold defense of themselves and obviously gain the crowd's favor, the rulers release them, though not before they threaten them if they do not remain silent. Upon returning to their own and reporting to them the happenings at the trial, the believers all joined in prayer.

> Sovereign Lord, who made the heaven and the earth, the sea, and everything in them, it is you who said by the Holy Spirit through our ancestor David your servant: "Why did the Gentiles rage, and the peoples imagine vain things? The kings of the earth took their stand, and the rulers have gathered together against the Lord and against his Messiah." For in this city, in fact, both Herod and Pontius Pilate, with the Gentiles and the peoples of Israel, gathered together against your holy servant Jesus, whom you anointed, to do whatever your hand and your plan had predestined to take place. And now, Lord, look at their threats, and grant to your servants to speak your word with all boldness, while you stretch out your hand to heal, and signs and wonders are performed through the name of your holy servant Jesus. (Acts 4:24–30)

In this prayer, the believers recite back to God part of a psalm he originally had spoken "by the Holy Spirit through David," namely Psalm 2:1–2. They follow this recitation with an interpretation, still within the context of prayer. This interpretation of Psalm 2:1–2 in Acts 4:27 is a classic example of the type of exegesis we discussed above and would fit very well among the Qumran pesherim. The believers' prayer interprets the opposition against God and God's anointed (*christos*) in Psalm 2:2 as opposition against Jesus, the one whom God anointed (*chrio*, Acts 4:27). This opposition resulted, by God's plan (4:28), in Jesus' execution.[31] Moving beyond the obvious, those praying find other verbal triggers in Psalm 2 that they see as pointing toward Jesus' execution. Hence, in Acts 4:27 the "kings" of Psalm 2:2 find their representative in Herod, whereas the "rulers" find theirs in Pilate. The raging "gentiles" (or "nations," *ethnē*) become the Roman soldiers who carried out the execution, and the "peoples" are the "peoples of Israel."[32]

The reason for including the psalm in their prayer is that because it accurately foretells what would befall Jesus, down to the parties involved, it shows that everything happened according "to…whatever your hand and your plan had predestined to take place" (4:27–28). Hence, the apostles pray to this God who exercises such control, asking that as they face threats of their own he will grant them "to speak your word with all boldness" (v. 29).[33] Not only this, they also ask God to continue the healings, signs, and wonders he performed through Jesus and to do so through Jesus' name (v. 30). To this prayer God provides God's own "amen," an earthquake and Spirit-filled proclamation (v. 31).

But is this simply a case of a pesher-style reading of the psalm without concern for its original setting, form, and function? A consideration of Psalm 2 demonstrates that whether intentional or not, it is a very appropriate prayer for the apostles as they take up the mission of Jesus and play out their own part in God's plan.[34] The second psalm, which—with Psalm 1—serves as an introduction to the Psalter, originally was a royal psalm. It was likely situated in a celebration of the enthronement of the king (Ps. 2:6: "I have set my king on Zion, on my holy hill"; 2:7: "You are my son; today I have begotten you"). The psalm is a dramatic description of the chaos that ensues at the transition from one ruler to another and of the sovereignty of God that stands against and vanquishes that chaos.

The description takes place in three movements. Verses 1–3 provide the psalmist's incredulous description of the vassals who seize the opportunity of transition to rebel against the Lord and his anointed: "Let us burst their bonds asunder, and cast their cords from us" (v. 3). Psalm 2:4–9 moves from the courts of worldly kings to the heavenly court, where God laughs derisively at the opposition. From this perspective, all the rebelling nations can do is incite God's wrath because certainly they cannot unseat the one he has established upon holy Zion (vv. 5–6). The king they would defy is "his son" who has but to ask and God will give him the entire world as his possession (vv. 7–8). This is bad news for the rulers, because God intends that this king "shall break them with a rod of iron, and dash them in pieces like a potter's vessel" (v. 9). The third movement, verses 10–12, is a direct address to the opposing rulers, calling on them to be wise and to be warned; they must submit to YHWH (to serve him "with fear" and "with trembling kiss his feet," vv. 11–12)[35] or else perish from God's quick-kindled wrath. The psalm ends with a note of reassurance ("Happy are all who take refuge in him") that seems to me to be directed at the Israelite audience who, overhearing YHWH's reaction to the agents of chaos, should take heart and put their trust in him.

Beyond what the prayer in Acts 4 highlights, our analysis reveals a number of other points of connection between Psalm 2 and the apostles. First, the apparent setting of the psalm, the transition of power, seems apropos. Acts 3:1–4:22 describes the apostles' experience as they took up Jesus' mantle and in like fashion encountered opposition from the same forces that opposed him. The apostles find themselves to be "newly installed" leaders who have encountered their first opposition; they must decide whether and how they will proceed.[36] Though articulated differently, both they and the Israelite king of Psalm 2 recognize that God is in charge and that they rule by God's power and authority. As God establishes and empowers the king in Psalm 2, so God endows and works through the apostles. The apostles also have the added security of knowing that as Jesus ultimately prevailed, so will they because they advance forward in his name.

The second point of connection is the irony inherent in both the psalm and Acts. Patrick Miller points out that, in Psalm 2, "the affairs of the small state of Judah are claimed to be of universal and cosmic scope." Of course, it is an "audacious presupposition of the psalm…that the tiny kingdom of Judah in southern Palestine and its king and God could claim ultimate power over all the nations of the earth."[37] Nevertheless, the psalm and those who worshiped by it so claimed. For Acts, the irony is in the Spirit-filled boldness by which the apostles proclaim the word of Christ. Luke highlights this in Peter's and John's trial before the Jewish rulers in 4:13: "Now when they saw the boldness of Peter and John and realized that they were uneducated and ordinary men, they were amazed and recognized them as companions of Jesus." Just as peculiar as the image of Judah lording it over the superpowers of Assyria and Egypt is the image of the unlettered and ordinary Peter and John holding their own against the erudite temple establishment.

Finally, the third point of connection is that Psalm 2 is programmatic for the story of Acts in general. Acts 3:1–4:22 is but the first in a series of instances of opposition between the apostles and the Jewish establishment. In Acts 5, the temple authorities will again place the apostles on trial and will consider more harsh means of putting an end to their movement. This is where the Pharisee Gamaliel counsels them: "[K]eep away from these men and let them alone; because if this plan or this undertaking is of human origin, it will fail; but if it is of God, you will not be able to overthrow them—in that case you may even be found fighting against God!" (Acts 5:38–39; cf. the rulers in Ps. 2). Such plotting and resistance does not stop, however, but continues throughout Paul's missionary journeys and his final visit to Jerusalem. Once he enters into the Roman judicial system, described in Acts 22–26, he follows in the path of his Lord by becoming a victim of collusion between the Roman governors and the Jewish leaders.[38] Hence, throughout Acts Luke describes how "the nations rage and the peoples plot vain things." The assurance Psalm 2 provides is that God is more than equal to all of this plotting. Luke perceives this, demonstrating frequently how God appropriates opponents' plots into God's own plan, bringing God's will out of their ill will. This is even more satisfying than the derisive laughter of the deity and is certainly reason to understand why "Happy are all who take refuge in him."

If Hebrews helps us to hear Psalm 95 speak God's unsettling voice, the prayer in Acts 4 helps us perceive the stabilizing security of God's purpose expressed in Psalm 2. The chaos, irony, and conflict that both Acts and the psalm attest should be familiar; they seem to be what necessarily occurs when people of faith live outside the will of a dominant and domineering culture. Finding that God not only mocks that culture derisively but consistently appropriates its best efforts (that is to say, its worst efforts) into the divine sovereign will, one cannot but help be reassured about choosing God's side and doing God's bidding. Those praying in Acts 4 saw in Psalm 2 a pattern of divine trustworthiness that had played itself out in the life, death, and resurrection of their Savior and was now doing so in their own experiences. Such trustworthiness should embolden all people of faith to respond in kind—as it did then: "[T]hey were all filled with the Holy Spirit and spoke the word of God with boldness" (Acts 4:31).

"My God, My God, Why Have You Forsaken Me?"
Psalm 22 in Mark 15

One of the most important advances critical Psalms scholarship has made is in the development of the lament genre. Exploring the Psalms that fit within this literary form has created an invaluable nexus between theological inquiry and human suffering. The belief that the Psalms are divinely inspired and at the same time include among their number Psalms that rant at God and plead with him creates a happy mystery, a divine embrace of our often dark and desperate emotional nature.[39] Because the fruit of this scholarship can be so affirming and so valuable, the approach of interpreting the Psalms typical to the ancient world can be so disheartening. Neither the Qumran pesher nor the patristic allegory, for instance, recognizes the nexus between theology and emotion. And the Psalms are rendered less human because of this.

It is not so much that ancient exegetical methods deny the emotional honesty of the text as it is they unduly circumscribe that honesty. Within early Christian circles, lament Psalms became expressions specifically of Christ's suffering.[40] While such application cannot but help to improve our appreciation for the Savior's passion, making laments of the words of Jesus risks taking them away from believers in general. The Savior, who alone was perfectly righteous, could cry out to God for abandoning him; how can we, so less noble, so much more imperfect, dare to speak as bluntly to God? With this in mind, the modern interpreter has reason to approach Mark 15 and its appropriation of the lament Psalm 22 with some reservation.

The cry "Eloi, Eloi, lema sabachthani?" in Mark 15:34 may capture the *ipsissima verba* of Jesus. If so, these words represent Jesus "as profoundly discouraged at the end of his long battle because God, to whose will Jesus committed himself at the beginning of his passion (Mk. 14:36; Mt. 26:39, 42) has not intervened in the struggle and seemingly left Jesus unsupported."[41] The cry itself is an Aramaic rendering of Psalm 22:1, "My God, my God, why have you forsaken me." Regardless whether this citation was the catalyst or the main result, it is clear that Psalm 22 shaped the Markan passion narrative.[42]

Psalm 22 is a personal lament that captures the essence of that genre by describing the alienation the psalmist experiences from God, others, and himself, doing so with an "unusual" intensity of feeling.[43] In the first part of the psalm (vv. 2–12, NAB)[44] the psalmist laments the contrast between his current dire circumstances and God's past faithfulness. He observes that where his ancestors trusted in God and were not disappointed, he calls "by day, but you do not answer; by night, but I have no relief" (v. 3, NAB). Though God drew him from the womb and has been his God since birth, he now sees himself as "a worm, hardly human." He is not alone in this perception of himself; those who pass him by, shaking their heads and mocking him, also share it.

The next section (vv. 13–23) shows his situation as worsening. The psalmist describes how he withers away physically:

> Like water my life drains away; all my bones grow soft. My heart has become like wax, it melts away within me. As dry as a potsherd is my throat; my tongue sticks to my palate; you lay me in the dust of death. (22:15–16, NAB)

At the same time he is wasting away, his enemies, a menagerie of beastly tormentors, are emboldened in their attacks upon him.[45] If only the Lord would come near.

> But you, LORD, do not stay far off; my strength, come quickly to help me. Deliver me from the sword, my forlorn life from the teeth of the dog. Save me form the lion's mouth, my poor life from the horns of wild bulls. (22:20–22, NAB)

Then a dramatic shift of perspective occurs in the remaining verses of Psalm 22. The next verses, anticipating God's saving action, contain the psalmist's invitation to praise the Lord. He himself "will offer praise in the great assembly; my vows I will fulfill before those who fear him" (v. 26, NAB), for "God has not spurned or disdained the misery of this poor wretch, did not turn away from me but heard me when I cried out" (v. 25, NAB).

The psalmist surprisingly expands the frame of reference at the conclusion of his psalm (vv. 28–32, NAB) to the scale of the universal ("All the families of nations will bow low before you," v. 28, NAB). Hence, he has moved from radical alienation with God and the world to a picture of universal reconciliation of all peoples. This will happen because "kingship belongs to the LORD, the ruler over nations" (v. 29, NAB). As Mays points out, the concluding vision of the psalm "is prophetic in character and eschatological in scope" because it shows how "[e]veryone–everywhere, of every condition, in every time–will join in the worship of those who recognize and rejoice that the universal sovereignty belongs to the LORD."[46]

In terms of Mark 15 and the execution of Jesus, we are only concerned with the lament or plaintive aspects of the psalm; the praise does not have any ostensible role.[47] As John Donahue and Daniel Harrington note, the lament aspect of Psalm 22 "provides a model or even a script for the story of Jesus' Passion and death."[48] Certainly there are plenty of overlapping themes: Jesus is alienated from God (hence his cry of forsakenness) and from humanity (his disciples have abandoned him and his enemies are emboldened). All the while his body is withering away (though by means of external forces more than internal distress). But the influence of Psalm 22, while more subtle than an outright pesher, is clearly palpable in Mark 15. There is, of course, Jesus' cry from Psalm 22:1. We also see literary traces of Psalm 22 in Mark 15:24 and 15:29. "And they crucified him, and divided his clothes among them, casting lots to decide what each should take" (Mk. 15:24) comes from Psalm 22:18: "[T]hey divide my clothes among themselves, and for my clothing they cast lots."

"Those who passed by derided him, shaking their heads..." (Mk. 15:29) comes from Psalm 22:7: "All who see me mock at me; they make mouths at me, they shake their heads." It is not surprising that some have argued the whole of the passion narrative functions as a *midrash,* an imaginative reinterpretation, of Psalm 22.

Why are this psalm and the passion so strongly associated? Perhaps the passion narrative, though more artistic and more subtle (by far), serves the same purpose as the pesherim; that is, it seeks to show that Psalm 22 has its fulfillment in the death of Christ and thereby reinforces that Christ's death is part of the divine plan. Such "recourse to the OT Scriptures" allows the gospel's audience "to make sense out of the cruel and shameful death Jesus suffered on the cross."[49]

But what about the cruelty and shame experienced by others? Tied to Jesus' experience and placed on his lips, does this lament cease to speak to the suffering of anyone else? Or better, does it cease to give them a voice to cry out to God in their suffering? Are other sufferers silenced when Jesus cries out? Before you say of course not, consider that the Christian interpretation and liturgical use of Psalm 22 comes to be solely associated with Jesus. Or as Mays describes it:

> Because of the close connection of Psalm 22 with Jesus, the custom developed in the early church of taking the psalm as Jesus' words and relocating it completely in a christological context.[50]

And again:

> The use of Psalm 22 in the New Testament and in the liturgy of Holy Week gives hermeneutical directions about the way believers are to understand it. We are given a role in the scenario of the psalm. We do not identify, either as individual or community, with the person who prays and praises, as in the use of many other psalms. That role is claimed for and explicated by Jesus alone.[51]

I am not suggesting that Mays himself sees this as ultimately isolating the sentiment of the psalm from sufferers other than Jesus. He understands how the biblical "prayer for help" quickens the prayers of believers who turn to the Psalter. Still, my experience has been that not everyone is as astute as he; many are like the early church, who came to see every personal lament psalm as referring to Jesus' passion. It does not help that people in our culture are inherently uncomfortable with lament. Giving Psalm 22 to Jesus allows many to continue to comfortably nurse their false sense of selves.

What is our response to this? We see the NT as authoritative, so we cannot deny Jesus his lament. Yet should we deprive— can we deprive—the laments to others? to ourselves even? I think our hope lies in the passion of Jesus. In a *Christian Century* article entitled "Vindication: The Cross as Good News for Women," A. Katherine Grieb seeks to correlate the violence of Jesus' crucifixion with the violence too many women have experienced.[52] She does so fully recognizing that many feminist scholars have eschewed the passion story as a narrative "dangerous" to women's health and well-being. Do women really need to emulate a violated victim? Grieb's response is to show that the following four reasons are why Jesus' death is still good news to women who have experienced violence.

1. The passion narrative does not blame the victim, as we so often do.

2. God's story—that is the passion narrative, honors the feelings of those who are violated; Jesus does not die well, he does not die the Noble Death, he dies screaming.

3. These feelings, however, are placed in their proper perspective: Though Jesus may have doubted that he was still God's beloved child, his bitter experience of abandonment was not the whole of reality—the reader is privy to what Jesus does not know.

4. God's story makes clear that people who are violated by others are vindicated by God. The crucified one is raised from the dead, lifted up, loved, and honored. Human atrocities are not the last word; they do not define us.

What strikes me as remarkable is that Grieb's reading of the passion narrative also functions as solid reading of Psalm 22 and of personal laments in general. If she is correct—and, of course, I think she is—the crucifixion of Jesus does not shut off the lament from anyone but him. Rather, his crucifixion—and his perfect ability to scream at God—opens up the floodgates of lament, providing as many as would turn to him the boldness, the right also to scream at God.

Conclusion

Clearly, when the NT preaches the psalms, it is to considerable effect. In the three passages we surveyed, we find ourselves confronted with fresh and challenging words from the Psalms. Hebrews opens our ears to God's piercing voice in Psalm 95; Acts draws from Psalm 2 to highlight God's pattern of trustworthiness in our chaotic world; and Mark liberates our humanity when the crucified Jesus screams the emotionally honest words of lament from Psalm 22.

It is perhaps surprising to find that the NT contains such powerful readings of the Psalms. After all, we cannot deny that, technically speaking, the NT authors approach the Psalms in the manner of their time and place. Furthermore, our own culturally conditioned training cautions us to eschew most of the principles inherent to this first-century exegesis. Yet from what we have just witnessed, it is evident that their exegetical methodology did not hinder the NT authors from astutely reading and faithfully relaying the message of the Psalms. This says something important about the Psalms and about the NT. With respect to the Psalms, they defy pedestrian interpretation. The Psalms relate a word of God that not only refuses to be domesticated, it makes uncommon demands of obedience, trust, and candor on any who dare to engage it. With respect to the NT, we find an authoritative example of deference to the Psalms. The NT passages we surveyed above do not co-opt the Psalms to their own ends; rather, they cooperate with those Psalms in seeking to admonish, inspire, and set free their audiences.

As in all things, we must allow the NT to guide us in preaching the Psalms. Following its example, we should use what skill and training we have to let the Psalms speak through us, trusting that our audience, even today, will hear God's voice.

6

Reading the Psalms for Preaching

Fictive Plot

PAUL SCOTT WILSON

A preacher who does not want to reduce the biblical text to mere abstract propositions and doctrines needs to find some way to honor the poetic form and function of the Psalms. They are songs written for occasions of sadness, lament (of an individual and of a community), and anger, as well as of joy, celebration, thanksgiving, and accomplishment. They are what Gerald Sheppard described as prayers "meant to be overheard by others."[1] They speak of or allude to all manner of human experience. Because many of these experiences are in the background, lacking precise profile, description, or historical location, they invite the preacher to bring contemporary experience to the text. Historical critical readings typically are not as fruitful as we might hope, for we cannot be sure who wrote which psalms, in what setting, to what purpose, or to what effect. Yet there is merit in not abandoning a diachronic focus too soon. The result may not be history per se, but it can be a narrative, literary, or fictive plot with a likeness to history that nonetheless opens important textual perspectives. The purpose of this essay is to go beyond a general suggestion that narrative is important in preaching the Psalms to suggest what might be the elements of that narrative.

The preaching of the church often has rendered the psalms using a narrative plot, yet the source of that plot has not always been a psalm itself. Psalm 3 serves as a good example, particularly as handled several centuries apart by Augustine, Calvin, and contemporary scholar J. Clinton McCann Jr., whose work I selected before knowing of his participation in this volume. Each of these scholars implies a plot concerning Psalm 3, and each has a different source of origin for that plot. I will first review each of their suggestions and then offer a fourth alternative of my own.

Of the seventy-three psalms that are said to be "of David," Psalm 3 is the first of thirteen that ascribes authorship to him during a specific stage in his life. The historical superscription reads "A Psalm of David, when he fled from his son Absalom." Ostensibly the Psalm opens a portal to events around 2 Samuel 15:17, yet what this has been interpreted to mean has varied widely.

Augustine and the Narrative Plot of Christ

Late in his life, Augustine compiled sermons to form the only complete commentary on the Psalms that survives from the ancient church, *The Exposition of the Psalms.* If one were to judge from his hermeneutical remarks in *On Christian Doctrine,*[2] one might predict that he read Psalm 3 using the literal or historical-grammatical sense, for scholars often note the priority he gives to it. As he says, some subject matters in scripture are meant to be taken literally ("openly"): "all those teachings which involve faith, the mores of living, and...hope and charity."[3] He says translations that opt for ambiguity (i.e., aiming at a figurative, nonliteral reading) when clarity is possible are wrong.[4] When in doubt, the "rule of faith" is to be applied, for it is the authority of the "greater number" of catholic churches that is preferred.[5]

However, when one turns to Augustine on Psalm 3, he immediately dispenses with the apparent historical meaning. David is a type of Christ. We forget too readily that for the church up to and including the Reformation, the literal sense was generally a double sense. The preferred higher literal sense was theological.[6] Augustine makes this move from David to Christ on the basis of verse 5, which he reads as Christ referring to his own resurrection: "I lie down and sleep; I wake again, because the LORD sustains me" (NIV). As Augustine says, these words "are more in keeping with our Lord's passion and resurrection than with the account which history gives of David's flight before the face of his own rebel son."[7] The historical setting of David with a disloyal son becomes a means for typological reflection on Jesus and Judas: "the disloyal son should be the figure [i.e., type] of the disloyal disciple who betrayed his Master."[8] This reading of the text, which treats the Psalm as foreshadowing the gospel events, considers Christ to be its higher literal sense; and the primary narrative plot in the Psalm is thus his life. Augustine continues to focus on the superscription, "'The Psalm of David when he fled from the face of his son Absalom…' From a literal standpoint one may say, it is true, that Christ fled before him when, on the departure of Judas, He withdrew with the rest to the mountain…This departure of our Lord, I think, is termed a flight in the Psalm on account of its swiftness."[9]

Augustine finds in some unnamed interpreters the name Absalom rendered in Latin to mean *patris pax,* "peace of his father." Here is his explanation:

> It may very well seem puzzling that the name, "peace of his father," can be appropriate…where Judas is the betrayer of our Lord. But a careful reader will perceive in the first instance that during the struggle there was peace in David's heart towards the son whose death he even bewailed with bitter grief: *Absalom my son!* he cried. *Would to God I might die for thee* [2 Sam. 18:33]. And when the history of the New Testament shows us the great, the truly wonderful forbearance of our Lord, who bore with Judas so long just as though he were upright,

and although He was aware of his designs yet admitted him to the feast in which He set before and entrusted to His disciples His own body and blood under a figure [i.e., a type], who finally in the other's very act of betrayal accepted his kiss [Mt. 26:49], we can easily see that Christ showed nothing but peace toward the man who betrayed Him, although the traitor's heart was prey to intentions so criminal. Absalom then is termed 'peace of his father' because his father cherished the peace which his son lacked.[10]

The primary plot of the Psalm, in Augustine's preaching, is the plot of Jesus' life; the speaker of the Psalm is not David or some other psalmist but Christ. As Augustine interprets verse 3, the words "But Thou, O LORD, takest me up" give insight to Christ's divine and human nature: "Christ speaks to God in His human nature, since God's taking of human nature is the Word made flesh."[11]

Calvin and the Narrative Plot of David

By the time we get to Calvin, the historical level of the text dominates, or at least how his age imagined that history from the chronicles of David's life. Calvin uses every opportunity to make links between the Psalm and David. The grammatical level of the text is also engaged, because Calvin knew Hebrew. He proceeds on the principle articulated by Melanchthon, "that Scripture cannot be understood theologically, unless it be first understood grammatically."[12] Calvin, at least for one period in his life, preached the Psalms on Sunday afternoons, the gospels on Sunday morning, and the Old Testament on weekdays.[13] Nearly everything he says is set within a theological context. He uses what opportunities he has to move into sermonic reflection in a manner that is still common today with preachers who expound their biblical texts verse by verse and apply each verse to the congregation. Scripture interprets scripture, thus obscure texts are clarified by less obscure ones,[14] and thus Samuel illuminates Psalm 3. Here are three portions of Calvin's commentary, starting with his commentary on the superscription:

A psalm of David, when he fled from Absalom his Son.

How bitter David's sorrow was under the conspiracy of his own household against him, which arose from the treachery of his own son, it is easy for every one of us to conjecture from the feelings of nature. And when, in addition to this, he knew that this disaster was brought upon him by God for his own fault in having defiled another man's wife, and for shedding innocent blood, he might have sunk into despair, and been overwhelmed by anguish, if he had not been encouraged by the promise of God, and thus hoped for life even in death.[15]

Because Augustine interpreted David to be Christ, he could not do what Calvin does here in reflecting on the depth of David's sin, yet even this sin Calvin turns into a testimony to the strength of David's faith that he could still hope for resurrection. Each time Calvin reflects on the text, he goes into the situation he imagines of David's life and emerges with theological and moral insight:

1. *O LORD, how are my oppressors multiplied! Many rise up against me.*
2. *Many say to my soul, There is no help for him in God. Selah.*

Sacred history teaches that David was not only dethroned, but forsaken by almost all men; so that he had well nigh as many enemies as he had subjects. It is true there accompanied him in his flight a few faithful friends; but he escaped in safety, not so much by their aid and protection as by the hiding-places of the wilderness…It was a mark of uncommon faith, when smitten with so great consternation, to venture freely to make his complaint to God, and, as it were, to pour out his soul into his bosom. [Here is Calvin's applica-tion:] And certainly the only remedy for allaying our fears is this, to cast upon him all the cares which trouble us; as, on the other hand, those who have the conviction that they are not the objects of his regard, must be prostrated and overwhelmed by the calamities which befall them.[16]

In his treatment of verses 3 and 4, Calvin brings a historical reading to bear on the Psalm. David is a real person, not a shadowy inaccessible person in the background but a man of genuine faith who is capable of receiving salvation. The words that Augustine put in the mouth of Christ are now placed in the mouth of David, who cries to God from his hiding place in the wilderness:

> 4. *I have cried to the Lord with my voice, and he heard me out of his holy hill. Selah.*
>
> ...As to the expression, *from the hill of his holiness,* or, which signifies the same thing, *from his holy hill,* it is improperly explained of heaven, as has been done by some. Heaven, I indeed confess, is often called, in other places, God's holy palace; but here David has doubtless a reference to the ark of the covenant, which at that time stood on Mount Sion...[Calvin cites 2 Samuel 15:24 as his evidence]. He knew that the Lord had chosen Sion to be the dwelling place of the ark...Now, he boasts, that although he was deprived sight of the ark, and notwithstanding the distance to which he was removed from it, God was near to him to listen to his prayers.[17]

Only at the end of Calvin's comments on verse 4 does he make a link to the life of Christ. He finds in the fact of David praying from the wilderness to God in Zion a theological awkwardness that is now remedied in Christ:

> Hence the confidence with which he [David] prayed; and this confidence was not without success. In our day, since there is fulfilled in Christ what was formerly shadowed forth by the figures of the law, a much easier way of approach to God is opened up for us, provided we do not knowingly and willingly wander from the way.[18]

Calvin still speaks of types and shadows, but in his treatment of this Psalm at least, Christological significance is left in the shadows. David's life as recorded by Samuel is the source of the narrative plot.

J. Clinton McCann Jr. and the Narrative Plot
of the Listener

We now turn to a contemporary scholar for yet a different narrative plot for Psalm 3.

J. Clinton McCann Jr. writes his commentary on Psalms in *The New Interpreter's Bible*[19] not as sermons; he simply addresses preachers and teachers with obvious keen sensitivity to their tasks. His introductory comments about the psalms of lament in general end up having relevance for many psalms that are not laments. He explains that while his commentary will note scholarly proposals concerning the possible historical origins of the laments, his emphasis will lie elsewhere, for this reason:

> [T]the language and imagery are symbolic and stereo-typical enough to be applicable to a variety of situations. While this may be a frustration to scholars who are attempting to pin down precisely the historical circumstances of a psalm's origin, it is a distinct advantage to faithful communities and people who actually pray the prayers and look to them for a word about God and their own lives under God…
>
> In other words, the really pertinent questions in approaching the laments are *not,* What was wrong with the psalmist? Who were her or his enemies? Rather, the crucial interpretive questions are these: What is wrong *with us?* Who or what are *our* enemies?[20]

McCann thus suggests that the real narrative plot in many psalms is the lives of the hearers. When he turns his attention to Psalm 3, he reinforces this. He pays no immediate attention to the historical superscription. He mentions it only in his concluding remarks, noting that it "should not be taken as historically accurate."[21] He distances himself from those scholars who take it as evidence that a king is praying and that Psalm 3 is thus a royal psalm. McCann shines the spotlight on the hearer's life:

> It is more likely that the superscription is intended to encourage the reader to imagine a situation like that of

> David's during Absalom's revolt. His family–indeed
> his life–was a wreck. Absalom had killed his brother
> Amnon for raping his sister Tamar (2 Sam. 13). David
> forgave Absalom (2 Sam. 14), but Absalom rebelled
> against his father and drove him from Jerusalem (2 Sam.
> 15). The whole sorry situation is illustrative of the messy
> situations we regularly experience–violence, turmoil,
> rebellion, threats to job and even to life itself.[22]

Apart from this significant reference, made less for historical
reasons than to prompt the reader's identification of contemporary situations the Psalm might address, McCann makes no
mention of David in relation to Psalm 3 in his commentary or
homiletical "Reflections."

For McCann, the speaker of the Psalm is not Christ, or
David, but an unknown psalmist. In McCann's actual
commentary we learn little about the psalmist, which is
presumably McCann's point: there is little to learn about the
real historical author. Most of the information that McCann
mines is obtained through linguistic, literary, rhetorical, form-
critical, and other kinds of analyses; but there is simply not
much accessible history behind the text. The foes in Psalm 3
are "opponents not only of the psalmist but also of God... They
trust no one but themselves and recognize no rule other than
their own.... Their words also reveal this intent: 'Don't look to
God for help.'"[23] McCann, elsewhere in collaboration with
James C. Howell, says, "Perhaps the easier entry point to a
Psalm for the preacher or for the reader is by way of an image."[24]
Use of an image is not fundamentally different from use of
narrative in that the image must be placed within a certain
narrative or conversational context. McCann in his commentary
highlights the image of God as a shield in verse 3 and the
confidence in the Lord in verse 4 that allows the psalmist to lie
down and sleep and wake again in verses 5 and 6. In contrast
to the unnamed opponents, the psalmist in verses 7 and 8 trusts
only God, calls on God for deliverance, and contradicts the
foes who say God will not help. McCann's homiletical
"Reflections" offer two strong preaching possibilities: (1) "God
helps those who cannot help themselves," and (2) "prayer is
for those who know they need help."[25]

In addition to the richness of these theological insights for preaching Psalm 3, McCann's commentary helps the preacher to see what the Psalm actually says by highlighting certain words and perspectives. In terms of offering a narrative plot that will assist the preacher, he has less to say than either Augustine or Calvin, which is not surprising because he confines himself to the Psalm itself and does not reach out to the life of David or Jesus. He directs the interpreter to contemporary life because historical knowledge is limited and because his own approach to the commentary is explicitly theological. As he says, "form criticism and rhetorical criticism have not yielded theological conclusions. It is sustained attention to the shaping and final form of the psalter that pushes the interpreter toward theological interpretation."[26] Two years before McCann's commentary, James L. Mays also went in the direction of the reader when he spoke about the identity of the individual in the Psalms: "But the individual *in* the psalm is not the same as the individual for whom the prayer was composed. The connection is not autobiographical or historical. The individual in the psalm is an instance of a type, just as the particular psalm is...The identity in the psalm is given to and assumed by the one who prays the prayer."[27]

A preacher conceivably might explore three quite different routes in going largely in front of the text with McCann: (1) Preach the critical approaches of his commentary. But this is a practice that presumably McCann and most authors of commentaries—indeed, most preachers—would find an appalling misuse of both biblical scholarship and the pulpit. (2) Preach the theological concept that McCann mines from the Psalm. This is a superb path to follow provided that the Psalm itself gets sufficient sermonic focus. If the Psalm is barely dealt with in a sermon or if a preacher moves too quickly to the hearer's lives, this suggestion can come dangerously close (a) to using the Bible as a mere springboard for one's own thoughts or (b) to what Hans Frei condemned as the Western practice of reducing biblical texts to propositions instead of allowing them to speak for themselves in their own way.[28] Were one to minimize the text of the Psalm, it might become mostly invisible, and its function to ensure that scripture guides the life of the church might be eclipsed. (3) Find the narrative plot of the Psalm in one's own or the congregation's life. This goal may be said to be the ultimate goal of homiletics, which aims for the Word to dwell in the life of the hearer. However, this has rarely been the initial goal of homiletics, which many would argue is first to open the text as a Word in which the hearer may dwell. Said another way, biblical preaching normally puts the spotlight substantially on the biblical text first and then shifts the spotlight to today. This may be done verse by verse, as Calvin on Psalm 3 demonstrates, or in a longer exposition-application format, provided one can find enough to say about the text.

An Alternative in Fictive Plot

A preacher needs to find some way to talk about a biblical text for a sufficient length of time such that the listener has an opportunity to hear it again, beyond its initial reading in the worship service, and can begin to discern and assimilate its distinct features. The preacher acts as a reliable guide, high-lighting this feature and that, reconstructing the text even in the process of interpreting it. Lecturing on the text is one possibility, speaking about it in abstract and propositional ways, stressing information perhaps over communication, though this seems more frowned on these days than it was some decades ago. Today, lecturing may not meet the listening and learning needs of the largest number and range of congregants. An alternative possibility that our above commentators demonstrate with Psalm 3 is the discovery of a narrative plot: Augustine turned to Christ, Calvin turned to David, and McCann points to the listener's life. Each did so on the basis of history: Augustine had no access to history as we know it and thus was encouraged to read the Old Testament as about Christ; Calvin wrote at the beginning of the Enlightenment and understood the account in Samuel to be historical; and McCann finds little behind the text and makes a postmodern move in front of the text in the direction of reader response.

Yet another possibility may be recommended that uses the biblical text at hand as the source of the narrative plot. This approach strives to be as historical as possible and uses the best insights of historical critical exegesis, yet it does not claim to be history. It produces what may be called a fictive plot. The word *fictive* relates to fiction and is connected with something that is literary and narrative; but as I use it here, it is not connected with something that is untrue or somehow disrespectful of the text. Rather, it honors the text by enhancing its features. By fictive plot I mean a plot that preachers discern in a biblical text and develop for their sermons. It is fictive in the sense that the preacher's own creative efforts are enrolled in the process of developing it. It is rooted in the biblical text and its history, yet it falls short of modern standards for history–it is more akin to history than being history. Hans Frei used the term *history-like* to describe biblical texts that employ realistic narrative,[29] and the fictive plot of the preacher is similarly history-like. Fictive plot is a vehicle for truth. Theologian Julian N. Hartt once said, "A story may be truthful, that is to say authentic, whether or not it is factually accurate. Which is to say it may square with our perceptions and value structures even though it may be faulted by our memories or by some public instrument for ascertaining the facts."[30] Hartt was speaking about theology, but his words may be said of the Psalms and of the preacher's attempt to render the truth of a psalm through the hearer's participation in it in the sermon. Said another way, fictive plot uses the best historical resources at hand to enliven the imagination of the congregation.[31]

When Hans Frei described biblical narrative as being "history-like," he plainly excluded "the Psalms, Proverbs, Job and the Pauline epistles" from this category.[32] His thesis was that realistic narrative has been ignored for its interpretative potential: "But in effect, the realistic or history-like quality of biblical narratives, acknowledged by all, instead of being examined for the bearing it had in its own right on meaning and interpretation, were immediately transposed into the quite different issue of whether or not the realistic narrative was historical."[33] What I am proposing is in a sense the inverse of Frei: that certain texts be interpreted in the sermon in narrative ways that render them history-like. If the product is not history, it is at least guided by the text at hand, has literary coherence, and is lifelike, rescued from potential abstraction. Because fictive plot is creative and is less-than-history, it does not pretend to be something else, and the preacher is not silenced by the constraints of history in speaking the Word.

What might be some of the features of the fictive plot of a psalm? We may name seven. First, it resembles the structure of the psalm itself. In this case Psalm 3 as a whole has a chiastic structure: The psalmist is in retreat at the beginning, reflecting both on the number of foes that "rise up against me" (v. 1, NIV) and on their words that "God will not deliver him" (v. 2, NIV). The psalmist's head is sunk low; yet when the thought that the Lord is his shield occurs to him, he finds his head is lifted, and he cries out to God. The middle of the Psalm is the crossover point: the psalmist falls asleep and wakes again, and he takes both the sleeping and the waking in safety as a sign that the Lord is sustaining, refreshing, and protecting him (v. 5). He awakens with renewed confidence in God, and thus he says that it will not matter if his foes number in the "tens of thousands drawn up against me on every side" (v. 6, NIV). In verse 7 he seems to rise up from his bed even as he calls on God to arise and strike the enemies–this is in balanced contrast to the enemies rising in verse 1. Finally, in verse 8, the psalmist who seemed close to exhaustion and despair at the beginning is now transformed and is bold and unwavering in his assurance of the Lord's deliverance and favor upon "your people."

A second feature of fictive plot is that it is free to use the historical superscriptions that are attached to one hundred and sixteen of the Psalms. They may not be historically accurate, and a sermon may acknowledge this; but because literary and theological coherence, not history, is the primary standard for fictive plot, the ascriptions can be accepted as adding to the richness of the Psalms. This use of the superscriptions is not to fly in the face of contemporary scholarship; Mays, for example, weighs the evidence for and against David as the psalmist in Psalm 3 before rejecting it.[34] However, it is to take seriously that the superscriptions are canonical even if some or all of them may be later additions to the original Psalms and even if they are not accurate as glosses on the texts. They represent links with other texts that some layer of biblical tradition chose to make and that various subsequent layers continued to support. The preacher is also free in many cases to cast the psalmist as David and so to reap enormous benefits for the congregation, not least in imagination and communication.

Listeners can readily imagine David and can less readily picture an unnamed "psalmist" about whom the preacher may seem to be distressingly coy in not naming. Further, by identifying David in Psalm 3, the hopeful note at its end is all the louder: We know something of the victory David found out of his despair, but we do not know anything about what one unnamed psalmist may actually have found out of his.

Third, in fictive plot the preacher uses whatever historical details are available to make—as much as is possible with just words—a movie, and not an essay, of the biblical text.[35] Some details about the *Sitz im Leben* are available, for instance, concerning clothing, climate, weather, vegetation, farming and herding practice, economy, archeology and geography, liturgical ritual, and pilgrimages to the Temple, and so forth.[36]

Fourth, in fictive plot the preacher bends details in the text to the perceived plot line. Although this may be interpreted to read into the text something that is not there, it can also be seen as a way of highlighting details that indeed are in the text to give them visibility and to give the text coherence and unity as a whole. For example, we bent details to the plot line when we attributed to David exhaustion, near despair, and being overcome by sleep in the early verses of Psalm 3. We bend them again when David awakens with renewed confidence, reading behind his cry for God to arise, David's own arising from his bed to face a new day. These same textual details might render a different fictive plot on another occasion or in the hands of another preacher, yet this variation of interpretative emphasis may be found with any interpretative process.[37] Another example of bending textual detail to plot can be demonstrated with verse 3, which reads, "But you are a shield around me, O LORD" (NIV). To highlight that image the preacher may choose to depict David as a soldier who finally comes to rest, alone and in retreat, and who in gazing at his shield (or, alternatively, in looking for and not finding his shield at his side) is reminded of God's protection as a shield.

Fifth, in creating the fictive plot the preacher of psalms designated to be "of David" may allude to circumstances in David's life. In Psalm 3 one may allude to those events that McCann mentions—a daughter raped, the rapist son murdered, the favorite avenging son out to kill the father–but one need not be limited to only that period to which the Psalm's superscription seems to point. One may go to any other aspect of David's story in the Bible with which a link or typological echo may be heard. Such connections can serve to make David more lifelike, his troubles all the more vivid, and God's protection all the more profound, provided these intertextual links do not dominate and drown out the particular psalm being preached. Indeed, the preacher might even allude to some aspect of Jesus' story[38] that links with David's, though perhaps only after the psalm has been heard with its own integrity, in its own time and setting as much as possible. One might even dare to hear the echo Augustine heard of Jesus' resurrection in David's sleeping and rising again, or one might find in the Psalm words that Jesus certainly prayed and may well have said in reference to his own life, yet one would need to stop short of saying that this Psalm is actually written about Christ. When such elements are woven into the fictive plot, they help to teach more than the Psalm to the congregation, they help to teach the Bible and the larger Christian faith and story.

Sixth, the fictive plot need not be high drama; indeed, it ought not be more than the text itself suggests. What we have found in Psalm 3 in one sense barely ranks as drama: David goes to sleep and rises with new hope. It is a brief episode in the life of David when the stakes were high, one time of desperately-needed sleep and refreshment; yet it contains more drama than first appears. In the pulpit on Sunday this one moment becomes the lens with which the congregation may view the dramatic events in both David's life and in the larger meta-narrative of the faith to which it connects through various echoes and types in the biblical story as a whole. Moreover, this one text becomes a lens through which listeners view their lives. The fictive plot thus becomes a plot of the listener's life, and that is usually more than enough drama for most people to cope with in the sermon time.

Seventh, and finally, the key player in fictive plot as we devise it is not David or any other named or unnamed psalmist. The key player is God. When the church reads the Bible as scripture, it reads for a Word that is from, about, and embodying

God in one instance, and about humanity's relationship to God in another. As James Mays says of the Psalms, they "are the poetry of the reign of the Lord."[39] The fictive plot of a psalm in summary form does not constitute the theme sentence of a sermon because it is just a string or progression of events. Were a preacher to try to use the plot summary in this manner (for example, "David falls asleep and rises, strengthened in his courage"), the sermon might lead this way and that without a clear sense of theological purpose. The fictive plot needs a theological focus or theme. This is provided by what the psalm says about God, or what I call the God sense of a text.[40] In Psalm 3, I like McCann's suggestion "God helps those who cannot help themselves." Other possibilities might include "God shields God's loved ones," or "God delivers the needy." As the preacher develops the fictive plot through the sermon as a whole, this theme sentence is inserted in numerous and various places, exactly as stated as well as in other words. This strategic repetition helps to ensure that both the psalm and the sermon arrive at the intended theological outcome.

The goal in this chapter has not been to characterize how three commentators from widely different eras treat biblical texts, but has rather been a limited demonstration of how they each treat Psalm 3 in one location in their writing. The goal also has not been to claim the practice of what I call fictive plot to be unique or innovative; preachers on the Psalms may follow something quite close to it without naming or describing it.[41] Certain principles of fictive plot may apply to other biblical genres that yield little by way of history, and that, too, is beyond the focus here. The goal has simply been to name fictive plot and to highlight its distinctive features and its advantages in dealing with a particular psalm that has little historical background. Fictive plot is distinct, first, in claiming the ways it is rooted in history yet is history-like and not history, and second, in valuing its own creative component, guided as it is by the structure of the text. Each of the other approaches had its own unacknowledged creative elements, but none was strictly historical either: Augustine thought he was being historical when he found Christ as the higher literal sense of the Psalms; Calvin thought he was being historical when he spoke about this Psalm in David's life; and McCann thought he was being faithful to history by denying much historical meaning behind the Psalm. Fictive plot merely honors the text as it own kind of history and does not claim to yield historical truth in the first instance so much as theological truth—and it provides only one possible route to that.

PART TWO

Sermons on
Performing the Psalms

7

Like a Child at Home

Psalm 23 and John 10:1–10

J. Clinton McCann Jr.

Introduction

As Walter Brueggemann points out in the first chapter in this volume, the book of Psalms includes numerous "little narratives," including "the narrative of a sheep." The following sermon attempts to hear Psalm 23 as "the narrative of a sheep." The goal is to "defamiliarize" a psalm that may be, to use Brueggemann's terms again, "too familiar." The point, as suggested in the sermon itself, is not to replace the traditional understandings and uses of Psalm 23, but rather to extend its range. My hope is that Psalm 23 will be understood not only as a "funeral psalm" for situations involving death and dying, but also as a psalm that informs our everyday life and living.

To this end, "the narrative of a sheep," which features God as the central character and fundamental reality of life, is a counter-narrative to what Brueggemann identifies as the "bad narrative" or "thin narrative" of consumerism, represented by the mall and expressive of a life of self-centeredness and greed rather than obedience and joy. As I point out in my essay in this volume, contemporary philosopher James Edwards suggests that the mall is the paramount symbol for modern life in North America. In short, "shopping unabated" is the predominant narrative of our life-stories.

As the sermon proposes, to receive life as a gift from God is to begin to reperform our lives, thus escaping the dangers posed by a mall-oriented lifestyle and the ideology of consumerism—addiction, boredom, conformity, and greed. Thus, we are liberated to take our place in God's household with all God's children—in Brueggemann's terms, "situated in the matrix of this old, long, deep community." In other words, to be led by the Good Shepherd means to be led beyond ourselves to rest in a place of "new obedience and a new joy," or to use the words of Isaac Watts in his hymn based on Psalm 23, which I have borrowed for the title of the sermon, to be led to a place where we can be "like a child at home."

Like a Child at Home

Northminster Presbyterian Church—Roswell, Georgia
March 16, 2003

"There is power in the twenty-third Psalm!" These words were spoken one morning during a field education seminar at Eden Seminary several years ago. The speaker was David Spooner, who for years had served as the chaplain at the Regional Medical Center and who had spent many hours with people in crisis—desperately ill people and families of those who were near death or who had just died. Out of this experience with people in crisis, David had discovered what he shared that morning: "There is power in the twenty-third Psalm!"

I am sure that if time permitted this morning, many of you could offer personal testimony about a critical time in your life when the twenty-third Psalm was a powerful force—perhaps at the funeral of a friend or loved one, or perhaps when you yourself faced squarely the reality of death. Without a doubt, Psalm 23 is a powerful comfort in the face of extremity, threat, and death. You already know that, which is why Walter Brueggemann says that it is almost pretentious to comment on the twenty-third Psalm. At the risk of being pretentious, though, I want to talk about Psalm 23 this morning; but I want us to consider another aspect of Psalm 23–not to replace the old, but rather, as it were, to extend the range of Psalm 23, so that we can claim Psalm 23 not just for times of extremity and death, *but also for our living every day!*

The fame and familiarity of the opening profession of trust may mask its radical nature: "The LORD is my shepherd, I shall not want." Or better translated, "The LORD is my shepherd, I shall lack nothing." To appreciate the depth and breadth of this profession, we really have to try to hear Psalm 23 like a sheep. For a sheep, to "lie down in green pastures" means to have *food;* to be led "beside still waters" means to have water to *drink;* to be led in "right paths" means not getting fatally lost or attacked by a predator. In short, says the psalmist, what a good shepherd does for his or her sheep, so God does for me: God "restores my soul," or better translated, God "keeps me alive"! Life is God's good *gift* to us; or we might say, God is the truly basic necessity of life.

Jesus reinforces that good news when he claims the role of the good shepherd in John 10. In Jesus Christ, as the opening chapter of John's gospel suggests, we see God incarnate; we see that the power behind the universe knows us "by name" (Jn. 10:3) and intends that we "have life, and have it abundantly" (10:10). "The LORD is my shepherd," so I have what I need. God is the truly basic necessity of life.

This is a radical profession, so radical in fact, that we are hard-pressed to believe it, especially in our cultural context that constantly encourages us to live *not* by the gracious provision of God, but rather by our own ingenuity and cleverness and hard work. Actually, the traditional translation of verse 1 may help to emphasize the radicalness of the profession, when we hear the word *want* in its contemporary sense of "desire" rather than the older sense of "lack nothing": "The Lord is my shepherd, *I shall not want"*–that is, I will not want anything more, because I have all I *need*.

You see, our culture systematically teaches us to *want* just about everything! Clinical psychologist and best-selling author Mary Pipher calls you and me "the 'I-want' generation."[1] One of my students last semester discovered a sweatshirt that is sold at the Mall of America and illustrates the mind-set that often prevails among us. The sweatshirt reads:

> Though I walk through
> The Mall of America
> I shall fear no evil;
> For with time and plastic
> In my pocket
> There's nothing to fear anyway.[2]

Mary Pipher suggests that this mentality is driven by advertising, which she calls our real "national religion."[3] To give you just one example, listen to part of this ad for a nationwide messaging system:

> You said it when you got your microwave oven,
> > Your answering machine,
> > > Your VCR,
> > > Fax machine,
> > > CD player,
> > > Cellular phone,
> > > Laptop computer,
> And every day, hundreds of thousands of people say it about SkyTel:
> "How did I ever *survive* without it?"

The ad continues: "Ask any business traveler who has SkyTel nationwide messaging to tell you about life without it. You'll hear about inaccurate messages, countless rounds of phone tag, and a long list of missed opportunities. Ultimately, you'll hear, 'I can't believe I *lived* without it.'"

What bothers me most about this ad is that none of the products it mentions existed when I was a child. Now, I may be old, but not that old! But, of course, this highlights the point that the advertisers want to make–that is, amazing luxuries are becoming so commonplace that we are encouraged to view them as basic necessities that we cannot live without! How incredibly radical it is for us to be able to say in the midst of this kind of setting, as a result of our trust in God, "I shall not want; I have all I need!"

Psalm 23 may well remind us of the advice that Jesus gave his disciples in the Sermon on the Mount in Matthew 6: "Do not worry about your life, what you will eat or what you will drink, or…what you will wear…But strive first for the kingdom of God and God's righteousness, and all these things will be given to you as well" (vv. 25, 33). Imagine that–not worrying about our lives! How much more peace of mind and peace of heart might we have if we accepted *enough as enough,* and quit worrying about getting more?! In other words, God is truly the basic necessity of life.

Now it's obvious that neither Jesus nor the psalmist meant that we should sit idly by and wait for a handout. That's not the point! The point is that both Jesus and the psalmist remind us that we ourselves cannot ultimately save ourselves. We cannot ultimately secure our own lives and our futures–our hard work can't do it; our accumulation of possessions can't do it; our dazzling technology can't do it. The only real and lasting security in death *and life* comes not from ourselves but from God. God is truly the basic necessity of life. "The Lord is my shepherd," and that's enough!

I heard a sermon many years ago in which the preacher suggested a sort of spiritual exercise or discipline that probably helps to put us in touch with the profound profession of trust that we find in Psalm 23. It is sort of the opposite of the power of positive thinking. He said that we Christians should regularly imagine the *worst* possible thing that could happen to us. We should do this, he said, not as a way of being negative or defeatist or morbid, but rather as a way of being realistic, and as a way of affirming our trust that even in the worst possible circumstance, God will be sufficient for our lives and for our future.

The good news of Psalm 23 and the good news of Jesus Christ is that it is possible to walk with hope through "the darkest valley," because we know that we are not alone. "You are with me," the psalmist says to God. As we face death *and life,* God is with us! And furthermore, because our lives belong to God and not simply to ourselves, *we are also with one another.* Notice where the psalmist ends up in Psalm 23—at "a table" in "the house of the LORD." In other words, the psalmist finds a place in the household of God, the family of God—or we would say, the church!

The final stanza of Isaac Watts's metrical paraphrase of Psalm 23, which we shall sing later, highlights beautifully this concept of God's household or home:

> The sure provisions of my God
> Attend me all my days;
> O may thy house be mine abode,
> And all my work be praise!
> There would I find a settled rest,
> While others go and come;
> No more a stranger or a guest,
> But *like a child at home.*[4]

The good news is...church is home! In her short story entitled "O Yes," Tillie Olson portrays Carol, a twelve–year old girl, and her mother as the only white people at a worship service in an African American church. They are there to see Carol's best friend be baptized, but the animated shouting and singing bother Carol. Her friend's mother tries to explain:

> "Maybe somebody's had a hard week, Carol, and they [sic] locked up with it. Maybe a lot of hard weeks bearing down."

> "Mother, my head hurts." [Carol responds to her own mom before the other mother continues]

> "And they're home, Carol, church is home. Maybe the only place they can feel how they feel and maybe let it come out. So they can go on. And it's all right."[5]

Church is home! Oh, I know that we church folk fuss and fight and frustrate one another regularly in a variety of ways. But at the same time, we know deep down that we need one another, and we know that sometimes we might not be able to take another step along life's difficult way without one another as visible reminders of the loving presence of the God to whom we trust our living and our dying.

The Lord is my shepherd, and that's enough! God is with us! And by the grace of God, we belong, first and foremost, now and forever, in God's own household…like a child at home! Thanks be to God! Amen.

8

Beauty

Psalm 27

JAMES HOWELL

Introduction

[Following Paul Wilson's features of a fictive plot, this sermon exemplifies the preacher who "bends details in the text to the perceived plot line." Not reading something into the text, the sermon holds one matter as central to Psalm 27:1–4: beholding the beauty of God in the temple. At the same time, the sermon's focus on God fits Wilson's concern that fictive plot see God as the central player in the sermon's fictive plot.]

This sermon was preached on September 27, 2004, for the seventy-fifth anniversary celebration of the marvelous neo-Gothic sanctuary of Myers Park United Methodist Church, where I had been the pastor for just over one year. The Psalter seemed the logical place to unearth a text for such a moment, and any of several Psalms could have been chosen for a sanctuary celebration.

The twenty-seventh Psalm recommended itself largely because I have been reading, thinking, and writing recently on

131

"beauty." Hardly alone, I am awestruck and strain to keep up with some recent, brilliant writing on the subject, most notably David Bentley Hart's *The Beauty of the Infinite*.[1] Not only have other theologians (John Milbank, Stanley Hauerwas, Rowan Williams, to name a few) treated "beauty" of late; in other disciplines, in both the humanities and science, "beauty" is an increasingly traveled avenue.

Looking at this sermon, I realize I was not taught to preach this way—but I wasn't taught to preach on the Psalms in any way whatsoever. Perhaps this sermon is like an archaeological trench dug into a tell. Some academics would demand that the sermon excavate the entire site, but we did a single trench, and in this sermon, we find one pottery shard, one hewn stone, maybe even a precious pearl, a single detail: "to behold the beauty of the Lord." In *Preaching the Psalms* (which I coauthored with Clint McCann)[2] we suggested the preacher has license to play with a single image in the Psalm—partly because of the rich homiletic tradition of doing so and partly because the Psalms themselves lift up images as windows into the heart of God.

Hopefully, the focus on the single shard (or pearl) will not blind the preacher to life in the larger tell. In the case of Psalm 27, we know something of the situation in which ancient Israel "beheld the beauty of the Lord." I had not thought of the effects of the sun striking the bronzed walls of the temple until I read Mark Smith's little introduction, *Psalms: The Divine Journey*,[3] but he reminds us that for Israel, the beauty of the Lord was manifested in the beauty of live moments in the Lord's house. So instead of framing a sermon around the entire Psalm, I zeroed in on a single detail, one that is exegetically and homiletically interesting, one that can be tied to the *realia* of Israel's life—and one capable of being tied meaningfully to the moment of today's sermon and the ongoing life of the church.

In a curious way, this sermon sits in a peculiar point in space, the space conceived by modern physics—a curved space, where two diverging lines may manage to meet out there someplace. This sermon looks behind and before the text, playing on the liturgical life and place in Israel that birthed the words of Psalm 27, but then the sermon also looks out ahead to the afterlife of the words, life and place, thinking of more sanctuaries, more liturgical settings, more people gathering, more beauty, ultimately linking us to them, the text taut as the rope holding us together.

Beauty

Myers Park United Methodist Church—Charlotte, North Carolina

September 2, 2004

As the climax to the harvest, perceiving life had just been extended by the sheer grace of God, pilgrims gathered in great caravans for the journey up to Jerusalem to offer sacrifice, thanksgiving, and praise. Along the way, they would sing psalms in anticipation of their glorious meeting with God in the holy city. Imagine a band of two dozen weary travelers, scaling the crest of Mount Scopus. Just before sunset they are taking in the vista of Mount Zion's gleaming stones–and they fall to their knees to weep for joy.

The sight was stupendous: tents dotting the hillsides, smoke from hundreds of campfires circling heavenward, the pivot of it all Solomon's temple. A song was overheard: "Great is the Lord in the city of our God, beautiful in height, God in her citadels...Walk around Zion, count its towers, note its ramparts, recount to the next generation, 'This is our God forever and ever'" (Ps. 48, author's condensed version). The sounds and smells of a great throng, then the awful yelps and worse odor of animals slaughtered for sacrifice, trumpets blaring, cymbals crashing, torches held high, the formation of a splendid processional into the courts of the holiest building on earth, dancing, litanies, all on tiptoe, eyes straining toward the ark of the covenant carried aloft. More singing: "How lovely is your dwelling place, O Lord of hosts! My soul longs, indeed it faints, for the courts of the Lord" (Ps. 84:1–2). "Clap your hands, all peoples...God has gone up with a shout" (Ps. 47:1, 5).

The temple was designed as a paradise on earth, the garden of Eden revisited, the cubish structure a massive stone bridge into heaven, into God's royal throne room, studded with precious jewels, draped in the most exotic fabrics. All the senses were titillated. From the daily grind of a grey, subsistence existence, pilgrims were startled by the rush of what we may call a surplus of beauty. After a dark night in the temple precincts, the sun would rise in the east, the brilliant beams piercing the interlaced clerestory windows near the ceiling, striking not just a bare stone wall, but flashing against the gold plating on those walls, refracting through the jewels, dazzling the fabric hangings. Another awestruck lyric: "In your light, we see light" (Ps. 36:9).

Can you feel the theater in which today's Psalm was performed? "The LORD is my light...The LORD is the stronghold... One thing I asked...to live in the house of the LORD all the days of my life, to behold the beauty of the LORD, and to inquire in his temple" (Ps. 27:1–4). The temple was the zenith of beauty, incomparable in beauty, an architectural window into the very heart of God, who is not just beautiful; God is Beauty.

"Here is the church, here is the steeple, open the doors and see all the people." Children wiggle their fingers, and a parent smiles, thinking, "The church isn't the building; it's the people!" But the building! A structure, unique in style, dedicated in purpose: a church, this one in which you sit this morning, or the thirteenth-century cathedral at Chartres, or a white A-frame fixed between cornfields in the Midwest. A curious beauty about these buildings. During the great Depression, a little Baptist church in Oakboro, North Carolina, was blown down by strong wind. My grandfather and his neighbors marshaled a bunch of timbers and with their own hands built another bridge into heaven. Humble as a dusty storefront church in the inner city, that church, like every church, from St. Peter's in Rome to a converted factory in the heartland of China, another paradise on earth, perhaps in the same way my daughter's coloring is every bit as much "art" as a Rembrandt. Whatever the architecture, those who sacrificed to build no doubt shared the discovery of the medieval mason Tom in Ken Follett's *Pillars of the Earth:*

He had worked on a cathedral once. At first he had treated it like any other job. He had been angry and resentful when the master builder had warned him that his work was not quite up to standard: he knew himself to be rather more careful than the average mason. But then he realized that the walls of a cathedral had to be not just good but *perfect*. This was because the cathedral was for God, and also because the building was so big that the slightest lean in the walls, the merest variation from the absolutely true and level, could weaken the structure fatally. Tom's resentment turned to fascination. The combination of a hugely ambitious building with merciless attention to the smallest detail opened Tom's eyes to the wonder of his craft. He learned about the importance of proportion, the symbolism of various numbers, and the almost magical formulas for working out the correct width of a wall or the angle of a step in a spiral staircase. Such things captivated him. He was surprised to learn that many masons found them incomprehensible.[4]

The magical beauty of the church for those whose deepest (even if unacknowledged) desire is "to behold the beauty of the Lord" rests on what transpires amidst the walls, especially if Amos Wilder is right:

> Going to Church is like approaching an open volcano
> where the world is molten
> and hearts are sifted.
> The altar is like a third rail that spatters sparks,
> the sanctuary is like the chamber next the atomic oven:
> there are invisible rays and you leave your watch outside.[5]

The peculiar, fierce beauty of the temple, and of any sanctuary, is in "the invisible rays," in the words, in the Word: the contents of that ark that shamed every idol; the liturgy of the temple; the sung, prayed, and proclaimed Word in worship.

"One thing I asked…to behold the beauty of the LORD." Some amnesia has vacuumed out our sense of the beauty of the spoken word. Show me the money! We modern fools trust only what we see instead of what we hear, and our lives are thus impoverished. Mel Allen, who broadcast New York Yankee games on radio and then television, lamented the advent of television, feeling it rendered his words extraneous. He decided that television was "a medium in which both the broadcaster and the fan became lazy–the broadcaster because he had to let the camera do so much of the work and the fan because he did not have to use his imagination. Allen felt he had a less-intimate relationship with his viewers."[6] Allen's "soft, almost silky voice…brought the fan into the Stadium…and projected a sense of intimacy with the players. He would begin by painting a word portrait…Television would be different in many ways, not least of all for the athletes. In the beginning it seemed to bring them greater fame, but in time it became clear that the fame was not so much greater as quicker. More often than not, it evaporated sooner. As radio was an instrument that could heighten the mystique of a player, television eventually demythologized the famous."[7]

Our culture knows no real mystique. Everything is demythologized, and we cannot fathom intimacy with anything we don't have our grubby hands on. Yet a little reflection, some time of reminiscing, may jog our memory. Lately I have been asking people, "Tell me the five most beautiful moments in your life." At first, they lunge toward something they saw: sunrise at the beach, a rock formation in Arizona, Monet's garden at Giverny. But when I press them, they go deeper, and the most beautiful moments in life are inevitably when words that matter are exchanged. "I told her, 'I love you'–and she smiled and said, 'I so hoped you would'"; or "My father explained why he had left, apologized, and said 'I am immensely proud of you'"; or "The tests reveal that it is benign." The beauty in *Romeo and Juliet* plays on words exchanged across a distance, Romeo on the ground, Juliet on the balcony, longing, yearning, but not in possession. Love is like that: words spoken, sentiments overheard, thoughts expressed. The gospel is a word, words, the Word. We read. We listen. Somebody preaches, and we hold hands and pray with our eyes closed, believing the words are heard and treasured like pearls. In the beginning was the

Word, and to behold the beauty of the Lord is to hear the story, to utter dumbfounded praise.

Of course, those words that constitute beauty are not mere words. To Bible-toting critics, Jesus declared, "You search the Scriptures, thinking that in them you will find eternal life. But they are about me..." (Jn. 5:39, author's trans.). The proclaimer became the Proclaimed; the words make palpable the Word. When I was a child, a friend taught me to draw a stick figure on the first page of a clean pad of paper and then to draw the same stick figure in a slightly different position on page two, moving forward further on page three, until finally I had fashioned a little silent film of a stick man running the high hurdles, the breeze created by fanning swiftly through the pad a surprising bonus. The scriptures breathe on us, and we see a living, moving Word, the Son of God, our Savior, beauty in motion. Dostoevsky said there is only one truly beautiful face, and it belongs to Jesus. The wisest saints have contemplated and been on intimate terms with "Lord Jesus...Beautiful Savior." Augustine wrote,

> He is beautiful in heaven, beautiful on earth; beautiful in the womb, beautiful in his parents' arms, beautiful in his miracles, beautiful in inviting to life, beautiful in not worrying about death, beautiful in giving his life and beautiful in the tomb, beautiful in heaven.[8]

Hans Urs von Balthasar suggested that "Christ's life is the highest form of religious sculpture; it consists not only of image and word, but exhibits a tangible corporeality as well."[9] He added a crucial clarification: "Beauty includes the cross...not only using shadows, but embracing "the most abysmal ugliness of sin and hell by virtue of the condescension of divine love, which has brought even sin and hell into that divine art for which there is no human analogue."[10] Indeed, the eyes of faith see the most profound beauty in him who

> had no form or majesty that we should look at him,
>> nothing in his appearance that we should desire him.
> He was despised and rejected by others;
>> a man of suffering and acquainted with infirmity;

and as one from whom others hide their faces…
Surely he has borne our infirmities
    and carried our diseases…
But he was wounded for our transgressions,
    crushed for our iniquities;
upon him was the punishment that made us whole,
    and by his bruises we are healed. (Isa. 53:2b–3a, 4a, 5)

We are healed, and we are ourselves beautified. Our pock-marked, gangly selves are reshaped, transformed, and made lovely by this one most beautiful One. "One thing I asked…to behold the beauty of the LORD." Shockingly, we are privileged to look into the mirror and swear in ultimate humility that we see the image of God in our own eyes, faces, and body–and not just in ours alone, but in those with whom we gather for worship. We are, miracle of miracles, the body of Christ, and so we, too, are beautiful. Those who would seek the beauty of the Lord have the best chance of seeing that Beautiful Savior when we join our hands in worship and in compassionate service on the stage of God's good world. Teresa of Avila is reputed to have said,

Christ has no body now on earth but yours:
    no hands but yours,
    no feet but yours.
Yours are the eyes through which the compassion of Christ looks out on a hurting world.
Yours are the feet with which he is to go about doing good.
Yours are the hands with which he is to bless now.

The beauty of the church keeps getting a dirty old cloak thrown over it, though. We live in a cacophonous world of dizzying choices, three hundred cable channels, one hundred kinds of cookies, diversions beckoning, marketing gurus licking their chops; and we fall for the lie that "More is better," that a crammed-full calendar is better, that doing seventeen things today is superior to doing just three, that owning ninety-two gadgets is better than owning just five. But didn't Jesus scold Martha gently at dinner? "Martha, Martha, you are worried and distracted by many things; there is need of only one thing"

(Lk. 10:41). Mary chose the one needful thing—echoing the psalmist: "One thing I asked...to behold the beauty of the LORD." The Lord's beauty is the pearl of great price: If we ever behold it, we do not bother even to grab a coat before we dash after it, the screen door slamming unnoticed on our old life of endless choices. Only one thing matters, not seventy things.

God provides help in the lives of the saints. God wove Saint Francis, Dorothy Day, my grandfather, and your own faith heroes in their mothers' wombs, called them out of the chaotic world of consuming and into God's own heart where they asked for just one thing, to behold the beauty of the Lord—and as they reflect the glory of God, we see that beauty. John Navone spoke of beautiful lives as "goodness making a spectacle of itself so that it may be loved."[11] Perhaps this is why the stories of so many saints are preserved in stained glass: the colored glass is translucent, toning down the intense, direct light of the sun that cannot be tolerated by mere mortals, exposing the color, the density, the beauty of the light. The beauty of the Lord would overwhelm the spiritually sensitive; but the simple, practical behavior of Mother Teresa is accessible, believable, doable. If a diminutive, arthritic schoolteacher from Albania can spoon porridge into a hungry child's mouth and change the world, then maybe I, too, can make a difference. Maybe I, too, can mirror in some simple way the beauty of the Lord.

The archbishop of Canterbury, Rowan Williams, wrote,

> The beauty of worship, the beauty of holy lives, the beauty of lovely objects—none of these, as is so often said, is an end in itself. But that does not then mean they are a means to something else. They simply *are,* the overflowing of response, the super-abundance of love, and that is what is Godlike about them.[12]

Pilgrims on the journey, relentlessly seeking the beautiful, stopping at the window, tugged by the hunch that Beauty is here, in this place, in these faces, even in my own, the one thing I have been clumsily asking for all my life, the illumination to humanity through the ages: he is beautiful in heaven, in his mother's womb, in the cross, in heaven, yesterday, now, and tomorrow.

9

Though Mountains Shake in the Sea

Psalm 46

MARK LOVE

Introduction

Psalm 46 needs no translator for modern audiences. This sermon stands against the backdrop of the Iraq war, making preaching from this psalm effortlessly contemporary. More specifically, this sermon finds its voice in the immediate aftermath of the Abu Ghraib prison scandal, making it difficult to exempt our nation from the list of those who "roar and foam." It was my hope that Psalm 46 might provide the possibility of an alternative allegiance that would resist the chaos of war. The opening and closing refrain of the sermon frames this intent, "We are the people of the stream."

The framing image of the stream comes from the fourth verse, "There is a river whose streams make glad the city of God." The life-giving image of the stream stands in contrast to the chaotic forces of the deep, waters that roar and foam. This same contrast exists in relation to God, whose presence makes

Zion an unshakable place, and the nations who are in an uproar. Hopefully, these contrasts perform in the sermon.

My intention in every sermon beginning with a text is to let two questions guide the process. What in this text wants to perform? How can the sermon allow this text to perform on a contemporary stage? These questions are particularly important when preaching from the Psalms. As Walter Brueggemann's essay in this volume points out, the poetic character of the Psalms lends them to limit expression. As acts of limit expression, "the Psalms practice speech in ways that keep pushing the envelope beyond the already known to that which cannot be known until it is uttered" (p. 31). Psalm 46, with its scarcity of historical detail and density of imaginative language, begs for a sermon less interested in explanation and more interested in evocative exploration.

Though Mountains Shake in the Sea

Rochester College—May 24, 2004

Psalm 46

In June 1970 I waded with my father into the clear, cold waters of the Yamhill River and received the gift of Christian baptism. Those cold waters wound their way to Camp Yamhill's Inspiration Point from the mountains of the Oregon Coast. But their life-giving source was the pure headwaters of the kingdom of heaven. I come to you today as a person of the stream.

Psalm 46

> God is our refuge and strength,
>> a very present help in trouble.
> Therefore we will not fear, though the earth should change,
>> though the mountains shake in the heart of the sea;
> though its waters roar and foam,
>> though the mountains tremble with its tumult. *Selah*

There is a river whose streams make glad the city of God,
    the holy habitation of the Most High.
God is in the midst of the city; it shall not be moved;
    God will help it when the morning dawns.
The nations are in an uproar, the kingdoms totter;
    he utters his voice, the earth melts.
The LORD of hosts is with us;
    the God of Jacob is our refuge. *Selah*
Come, behold the works of the LORD;
    see what desolations he has brought on the earth.
He makes wars cease to the end of the earth;
    he breaks the bow, and shatters the spear;
    he burns the shields with fire.
"Be still, and know that I am God!
    I am exalted among the nations,
    I am exalted in the earth."
The LORD of hosts is with us;
    the God of Jacob is our refuge. *Selah*

We Will Not Fear

We will not fear. We *will* not fear. We believe better than
that.

We will not fear, even though chaos bubble up through the
cracks of our poorly ordered world and threaten to engulf us.
Because we sing better songs than that.

So, we will not fear—even though the earth should change—
even if someone should poke a hole in the ozone layer and
melt the polar ice cap, swallowing the dry land. We will not
fear.

Though the mountains shake in the sea, stirring the cauldron
of the deep, awakening the primitive depths and whatever dark
creatures lurk there. We will not fear.

Though the waters of the deep roar and foam and throw
themselves against the land, far beyond their appointed limits,
and threaten to swallow us and drag us into the churning power
of cold, liquid darkness. We will not fear.

Though the mountains tremble and quake, and rocks split
with ear-shattering thunder, and landslides descend to bury us
alive.

We will not fear. We *will* not fear.

Though trouble be everywhere about us, we will be people of courage, for God is round about us. We will not be dismayed. God is a very present help in trouble, our refuge and strength. We will not fear.

Though the Nations Court Chaos

We will not fear, which is a brave stance indeed, today. Because the nations rage. Maybe you've noticed. Even the fair and balanced news organizations are reporting it. The nations are in an uproar. Kingdoms quake.

The nations are courting chaos, hoping to load it into a warhead, to turn it into an invisible gas, to harness its destructive power, to maintain some semblance of control over the worlds for which they claim sovereignty. North Korea, Pakistan, India, Afghanistan, the Palestinians and Israelis, Iraq, Iran, Sudan: It's not hard to name places where the mountains quake in the depths of the sea, where the sea roars and foams.

This picture just destroys me.[1] I see this picture and I wonder, Is the trouble just out there? Or could it be in here? in me? I want to say that this picture represents the work of just a few bad apples. But my psychologist friends tell me that it's not the apples, it's the barrel. That when you put people—not bad, cruel, sadistic people, but our neighbors, seemingly nice, responsible people—in these kinds of positions, these results are inevitable. When you ask them to enter chaos, chaos enters them. The trouble isn't only out there. We have trouble right here in River City as well.

This picture touches that place in me that says the powers for chaos are always just beneath the surface.[2] That the world that we see is a world pulled down over our eyes. That from our birth, cold, impersonal forces cultivate us for their purposes. That the goodness within me is not nearly so big or strong to keep the world that I've constructed intact. That we have no mastery over the powers, but they have mastery over us.

It touches the place in me that fears that I've been reduced to a series of numbers, a combination of 1's and 0's, that swim everywhere around me, being sent in cyberspace back and forth in ways that I can't even imagine. That even if I can access my credit report, I can't keep people from Googling me, or snatching my credit card numbers out of thin air, or stealing my identity of all things, or reading my e-mail. That there is an abyss, a deep sea of code that is not just information about me, but information that controls me.

Don't get the wrong idea here. I'm not a conspiracy nut. In fact, it might be comforting for me to believe that an identifiable group was in control—an identifiable enemy that could be resisted and dethroned. My fear is that no one is in control. That forces beyond human sovereignty threaten to engulf us at every turn.

That not even the goodness of democracy can hold back them back.

That good and evil are concepts too facile, instruments too blunt to adequately divide our world.

That not even a president who prays can keep us from hooding men and attaching electrodes to their bodies.

The nations are courting chaos, the same chaos that is everywhere around us, and even within us. To say in a world like this "We will not fear" requires an appeal to powers above all of this. Powers beyond human sovereignty.

In Search of a Sacred Place

Don't you love quest movies[3] —you know, the ones where our intrepid heroes are in search of some sacred space or relic or combination thereof to stave off the powers of evil? If only our heroes can climb Mount Mordor and throw the ring of power into the boiling fires of evil. Or if only Indiana Jones can find the hiding place of the holy grail and pass all the requisite tests, then the blasted Nazis will get theirs. The quest is often in search of a place where all the powers of the universe come together—things above the earth and below the earth all come together in a sacred space to harness the power of the universe—usually just in the nick of time to save the earth from forces that would destroy it. And usually this salvation comes in the form of some kind of laser, or flesh-melting pillar of godly smoke.

Psalm 46 knows a place like this: The holy habitation of the Most High. Zion. The center of the universe. The place where heaven and earth, and those things under the earth, all come together. The great navel of the world, attached as it were by umbilical cord to the LORD of Hosts. The one who rules above all. Whose name is above all names. Who brooks no rivals. The one who directs the heavenly hosts. The one who not only is not subject to the powers of chaos, but is the one who created them and ultimately rules over them. And Zion is where God makes God's presence known in the earth. And on that mountain, there is no quaking, no knocking of knees–only power. Those who know Zion sing, "The LORD of Hosts is our strength."

Come, let's see what all the uproar of the nations looks like from the unshakeable mountain, from the perspective of the habitation of the most High. Let's see what quick work the LORD of Hosts makes of all of this. Look what desolations God has brought on the earth.

Desolations. Not a happy word. No one ever says, "Hey, honey, let's grab the kids and head out to the edge of the earth and watch the desolations." But desolation is what happens when the coming of the LORD of Hosts meets the roaring of the nations. God speaks, and the earth melts.

"Knock it off!" God roars from heaven. "Be still and know that I am God. Cease and desist. I am exalted among the nations, I am exalted in the earth. All this roaring and quaking is false bravado. I've got your jihad right here. I'll show you shock and awe. Be still, and know that I am God."

Look, you don't want to be found holding weapons when the LORD of Hosts comes. God will find them. God will break bows and shatter spears and burn shields with fire. God will chase war to the ends of the earth. Here is our strength. The LORD of Hosts is with us. We will not fear.

But let's not leave the view from the habitation of the Most High just yet. There's more to see. If we were to leave right now, we might carry with us the impression that the dwelling of the Most High is only a dark fortress, complete with eerie fog and lightning bolts. That the one who lives there is only raw and dangerous power.

But the place where God dwells, where heaven and earth come together in power, is a place of gladness. My hunch is that this is what caught your eye as we read our Psalm this afternoon: "There is a river whose streams make glad the city of God." Is there anything more refreshing, more life-giving than a stream? A stream-cooled breeze on your face. Renewing water washing over your feet and ankles as you stand in the shallows. The soothing sound of water over rock, saying, "peace." Calling your name. It's no wonder we sing, "Peace Like a River."

And this river makes glad the city of God. I don't want to talk out of school here, especially at a Church of Christ college, but the phrase "make glad" typically doesn't go with water in scripture. Let's just say that if you bottled this stuff, it wouldn't say Ozarka, but might say "Gallo," or even "Cana of Galilee," and would be more likely to have a cork than a twist-off cap. We're talking "make glad" here. Abundant joy. No rationing here. No lawn-watering restrictions. No fear that our enemy will cut us off from the life-giving flow of this stream or that it will be polluted upstream. For only God is upstream. God is the source of the stream. The God of Jacob.

The one we know as the LORD of Hosts we also know as the God of Jacob. God doesn't come to us only as earth-melting power. God is not simply a list of indiscriminate attributes–omnipotent, omnipresent. God is not simply power. God is personality. God is not like the ocean, power everywhere crashing upon the earth. God is like the river, power in a channel, power moving someplace. Not just power destroying, but power healing, refreshing, bringing life. God has made himself available to us in a stream, in a story, through a covenant, by limiting himself and making himself vulnerable. The LORD of Hosts is the God of Jacob. God has given us the refuge of a story that shows that God knows us, and through which we might come to know God in gladness.

So, we gather at the gladdening stream. We gather for family reunion. We gather to tell stories of the God of Jacob. To remember. To laugh until our faces hurt. To wipe tears of aching joy from the corners of our eyes. The stories are well-worn, like rocks in the stream. We tell the story of Abraham and Isaac and smile knowingly and say to one another, "God will provide." And when the stars come out, someone always tells the story of the heavenly visitor who wrestled with Jacob, who didn't destroy him but left him with a graceful limp. We feel safe when we hear that story, not only because we see God making himself vulnerable, but also because we know that God blesses and saves and works through the vulnerable. It makes us brave enough to tell our own stories and wonder whether or not the LORD of Hosts has wrestled with us as well. And with the soothing sound of the stream in our ears, we say, "the God of Jacob is our refuge."

But the stream isn't meant only for the habitation of God. Its waters bring life to all the earth. Wherever it flows, it brings life and peace. Wherever it flows, the ongoing work of God's creation resists the chaotic forces at work in the world. The stream makes glad the city of God, but it also brings life to the earth. This healing stream makes war cease to the ends of the earth and says to all who have ears to hear, "Be still and know that I am God. I am exalted among the nations. I am exalted in the earth."

We Are the People of the Stream

All things in heaven and earth and under the earth have come together in the habitation of the Most High. The LORD of Hosts has established his presence in the earth, and a river runs through it. Streams of power, power to bring life, to heal.

And we have waded into the stream—to know the strength of the LORD of Hosts and the refuge of the God of Jacob.

But more, we have waded into the stream to be carried into the world of God's concern. In the midst of a chaotic world, we have placed ourselves downstream from the unshakable place to be carried into the world in the power of the LORD of Hosts and to serve the peaceful interests of the God of Jacob.

Be assured of this: All of the earth—because it belongs to God—will know the power of the LORD of Hosts. When the morning comes, God will act on behalf of God's presence in the world; and all of creation will hear the declaration, "I am the sovereign Lord." How the world experiences that declaration may depend on how willing we are to be the people of the stream.

To be the story carrier of the one who makes himself powerful in vulnerability. To tell the story so well and with such passion that whenever we say "the God of Jacob," whole worlds leap into view.

To be those who know how to rejoice around the gladdening stream of God. To allow praise to establish God's reign in the earth. To train our tongues for blessing instead of cursing. To sing more than we know.

To be the people of the stream means we will refuse the world given to us by the powers of this chaotic age. Instead, we will embrace the power of the vulnerable one. To be the ones who refuse bow and spear and shield. To be God's patient people in the world, not always rushing around to serve our purposes, but resting in the sovereignty of God. To be the ones willing to walk in the world with a graceful limp.

Which is to be brave in the world. We sing today a song of courage. We will not be afraid. The sin today is to despair—to sing this song and then to live without courage. To despair in the face of the uproar of the nations, to take our eyes off the presence of God and find ourselves sinking into roaring and foaming waters.

The sin today would be to plug ourselves back into the Matrix,[4] to pull the world down over our eyes again, to pretend that we had never sung Psalm 46. The temptation to despair is especially strong for us, who live in affluence, who can use the thin veneer of the good life to convince ourselves that human ability is enough to hold back chaotic forces that threaten the work of God's creation.

The sin would be to lose heart and reduce our worlds to make them more manageable, and then to reduce our language about God accordingly. To over-identify God with our cause and subsequently to lose our sense of God's sovereignty.

But today we sing a better song, a song that will not allow us to collapse back into fear.

Though the earth should change, the seas roar and foam, the mountains tremble with its tumult. We will not fear.

Though the nations rage and the kingdoms totter, we will not be afraid. The LORD of Hosts is our strength.

Though the morning of God's help seems far away, we will not be afraid, because the God of Jacob is our refuge.

We are the people of the stream.

10

The Goodness of God

Psalm 73

DAVE BLAND

One of the amazing things about Walter Brueggemann's writings is the tremendous heuristic value they generate; his work spawns creative thought and imagination in those who reflect on what he writes. That is what happened to me as I read his latest collection of sermons edited by Anna Carter Florence.[1] As I read his sermon on Psalm 73, my mind began to imagine and re-create possibilities. Brueggemann's use of the before-and-after scenario in the sermon inspired me to implement that structure in my sermon on Psalm 73.

Brueggemann's chapters in this volume also possess the same heuristic value. In chapter 1, he advises preachers to transpose the Psalms into narratives and work to recover the narrative situation in which the psalm originated. Psalm 73 clearly has a narrative before-and-after flow that makes it easy to convert into a narrative sermon. The psalm describes the faith struggles the psalmist experiences along the way to entering

151

into a deeper relationship with God. Early in the journey the psalmist almost succumbed to the secular narrative of commodity, as Brueggemann describes it. Then he remembered the truth narrative of communion. It was that narrative that brought the psalmist into relationship with God.

Flowing out of the recovery of the original narrative of the psalm, Brueggemann suggests that the preacher identify a contemporary setting that corresponds to the original narrative and assign a superscription to the psalm. For example, Brueggemann imagines the following superscription to Psalm 73: "For Howard, child of privilege, one year out of Harvard, a CPA with bonuses for hiring, almost empowered beyond recall, but stopped short by the quotidian truth of his life in a family of faith."[2] Such provocative ideas hold great potential for preaching from the Psalms.

Not only is the following sermon indebted to Brueggemann's work, it also seeks to integrate the work of Clinton McCann. In this sermon, I work to incorporate the theological perspective McCann develops in chapter 3. One of the symbolic enemies that McCann identifies in North America today is the enemy of greed. This sermon attempts to develop that dimension.[3]

The Goodness of God

WHITE STATION CHURCH OF CHRIST—MEMPHIS, TENNESSEE

JUNE 27, 2004

Truly God is good to the upright,
    to those who are pure in heart.
But as for me, my feet had almost stumbled;
    my steps had nearly slipped.
For I was envious of the arrogant;
    I saw the prosperity of the wicked.
    (Ps. 73:1–3)

You've seen those TV commercials that use before-and-after pictures to promote their product. For example, a weight-loss program shows a slightly overweight man in swim trunks on one side of the screen (it doesn't take much to make you look bad when you're in swim trunks), and on the other side is that same man two weeks later who's developed washboard abs because he's on the miracle drug "slim dim." The before-and-after commercials present stark contrasts of the same person.

On occasion we witness the before-and-after scenario in our own lives. I know a woman who grew up in a dysfunctional family. Both of her parents were alcoholics. Later in life she found herself, in an amazing turn of events, serving as a counselor for families of alcoholics. I also think of the young man who grew up performing poorly in school only to find himself in his adult life as the author of a best-selling book and teaching in a reputable university. His parents often ask, "Is this the same person we raised as a boy?"

Psalm 73 reminds me of this before-and-after type of scenario. It presents a before-and-after picture of a person struggling in faith and in lifestyle. The psalmist begins by describing the before picture. The psalmist was a pious man keeping the Torah with thoughtful discipline and conscientiousness. Then he began to look around and notice that others who weren't quite as committed to God and to scripture were prospering a lot more than he was. They only tipped their hat to God and Torah, and yet they succeeded in everything they did:

> For they have no pain;
> > their bodies are sound and sleek.
> They are not in trouble as others are;
> > they are not plagued like other people. (vv. 4–5)

They live in nice homes; they drive the nice cars and eat at the finest restaurants. They own a cabin on the beach and usually spend a couple of weekends a month enjoying fishing and boating. Conspicuous consumption is the name of their game. These wealthy became so successful in what they did that those around them turned them into celebrities:

> Therefore the people turn and praise them,
> and find no fault in them. (v. 10)

Everyone admired them! They were treated like royalty! They got all the attention. They became so confident in their own successes that they even began to thumb their noses at God. "Relax," they seemed to say, "God doesn't control everything. He doesn't care about every little detail that happens on this earth!"

> And they say, 'How can God know?
> Is there knowledge in the Most High?'
> Such are the wicked;
> always at ease, they increase in riches. (vv. 11–12)

The psalmist is rocked with jealousy: "I want what they have. I want their lifestyle: their homes, cars, no-obligation weekends." He was so obsessed with wanting to live in luxury that he was about ready to call it quits with the disciplined life under God's Torah. This religious stuff wasn't getting him anywhere.

That's the before picture. The after picture stands in stark contrast! The after picture begins in verse 18 and develops through the end of the psalm. You can't help but ask, "Is this the same person?" Here, he speaks about his life from a totally different perspective. He is glad for his new identity. He looks back on the before phase and sees that he had really acted like a mad man, a "brute beast" (v. 22). But now, from this new perspective, he perceives the end of the wicked. He doesn't want to be like them anymore. They're not the kind of celebrities or heroes that he wants to emulate. All he wants is to be near God:

> Whom have I in heaven but you?
> And there is nothing on earth that I desire other than you.
> My flesh and my heart may fail,
> but God is the strength of my heart and my portion forever…
> But for me it is good to be near God;
> I have made the Lord GOD my refuge,
> to tell of all your works. (vv. 25–26, 28)

The psalmist comes to experience the reality of God's ever-present and undying care. The psalmist's whole life is wrapped in God's love.

That's the before-and-after picture. The psalmist moves from a desire to acquire commodities to a desire to commune with God. The psalmist had always believed that "God is good to the upright" (v. 1). But he had developed a false understanding of what it meant. He thought it meant that God would bless him with the good things of life—wealth and power and success. He now understands it from a new perspective. "God is good to the upright" does not mean that God is a cosmic bellhop doling out material gifts. It means, rather, that God is a parent who longs for a relationship with God's children in which God can express love and discipline. The psalmist discovers that God is good, but not in terms of rewards. Rather, it is good to be near God. Like a loving parent, the "good" God gives is not things but self. So the psalmist goes from a desire to indulge himself in the pleasures of life to a desire to live responsibly in the presence of God. The proof of God's goodness rests in divine presence and not in material prosperity.[4]

As wealthy Christians in America, we struggle with living in the "before" world of this psalmist. We are consumers. Materialism and greed are deeply rooted in our way of life. It's a part of our history and even our religious tradition. During the latter part of the nineteenth century, one of the best-known apologists for the gospel of wealth was Russell Conwell, who preached for a Baptist church in Philadelphia for forty-six years and became famous for his sermon *Acres of Diamonds*. Between 1900 and 1925 (when he died), he delivered the sermon five thousand times. In the sermon he makes this statement, "I say that you ought to get rich, and it is your duty to get rich. How many of my pious brethren say to me, 'Do you, a Christian minister, spend your time going up and down the country advising young people to get rich, to get money?' 'Yes, of course I do.' They say, 'Isn't that awful! Why don't you preach the gospel instead of preaching about man's making money?' 'Because to make money honestly is to preach the gospel.' That is the reason."[5] I do not deny that Conwell did wonderful things with his money. But in America one can engage in acts of generosity and still be greedy. His philosophy of making all the money you can influenced untold numbers of people. It's a part of our heritage.

Greed is a way of life for us. It is little wonder, then, that upon entering America's universities, relatively few students ask the question, How can I prepare academically for a life of service? Instead, most students enter the university with one all-important question: What can I choose for my major that will guarantee wealth, possessions, and economic security?

After the terrorist attack of 9/11, government officials from the top down told us that the most patriotic thing we could do is "go spend money."[6] That advice lends credence to Robert Bellah's judgment that "the economy is like a heroin addict; only another shot of the very profit narcotic that creates a recession will get us out of it."[7] Americans are addicted to wealth as a narcotic.

A group by the name of "Sweet Honey in the Rock" sings a song entitled "Greed." One of the stanzas in the song hits a real nerve:

> Greed is a poison rising in this land
> The soul of the people twisted in its command
> Greed is a strand of the American dream
> Having more than you need is the essential theme
> Everybody wanting more than they need to survive
> Is a perfect indication, greed has settled inside.[8]

Greed infiltrates our lives. It's the air we breathe. That's the before world of both the psalmist and us.

How do we break the grip that the world holds on us? How do we get to the after phase? It's not easy. It's not easy to move from consumer to communion mode. Yet the psalmist made the move. How did he do it? The psalmist experienced a turning point in his life; it was a moment of truth when life and scripture took on new meaning:

> But when I thought how to understand this,
>   it seemed to me a wearisome task,
> until I went into the sanctuary of God;
>   then I perceived their end. (vv. 16–17)

He entered the sanctuary of God. There, he was given a new perspective on his situation and on the fate of the wicked.

What happened in the sanctuary? Was it being in the presence of a worshiping community that resulted in the transformation? Did he receive some kind of revelation from God? The experience in the sanctuary remains unspecified. I speculate that it may have been both. Being with fellow believers and meditating on God's Word gave him a new perspective on life. God revealed to him a different way of interpreting the meaning of the words he'd been taught, "God is good to those who are pure in heart."

In the verses that follow his experience in the sanctuary (18–28), the psalmist returns to reaffirm what he had stated in verse 1, "truly God is good to the upright." Now he understands it from a new perspective. As Walt Brueggemann says, "Now that the psalmist is torah focused, new light is shed on the situation. What counts is not profit but presence; not success but relationship."[9]

The New Testament contains a narrative counterpoint to Psalm 73. It is the parable of the prodigal son.[10] The prodigal son's experience is strikingly similar to this psalmist's experience with a before-and-after scenario. In the before phase, the son wanted to experience the good life. So he took his inheritance from his father and indulged himself in the finest things of life. He wanted to have all the material goods the world could offer. That was the before picture: prosperity. The after picture alters the scene radically. Now all the son wants is to be in his father's presence, even if it means nothing more than being one of his hired servants. Communion with his father was the real meaning of life. How did he move from one lifestyle to the other? There is this striking phrase similar to the one in Psalm 73: "he came to himself" (Lk. 15:17). He experienced a moment of truth. We don't know what changed his perspective, but it was changed. His previous desire for wealth and prosperity was a dead end. He comes to realize his true identity: He is not just a slave, a hired hand, but a son loved by his father! He discovers the father's love. Then being in the presence of his father is the only thing that matters.

Philip Yancey tells about his friend who had a fifteen-year-old daughter. The daughter was rebellious. She had lied to her parents, was disrespectful, and some nights refused to come home. She blamed her parents for her predicament. The father told Yancey, "One evening I was standing in front of our picture window looking out waiting for my daughter to return. I was furious with her for the way she manipulated us. I could better understand God's deep anguish over God's rebellious people." Then the father said, "But when my daughter came home early in the morning, I wanted nothing in the world so much as to take her in my arms, to love her, to tell her I wanted the best for her. I was a lovesick father."[11]

God is heartsick and longs for relationship with God's people. When we come to understand how deep the Father's love for us is, we are transformed from people concerned with prosperity and commodities and profit to people concerned about communion with a God whose steadfast love never ceases.

11

Going to Church in the Psalms
Psalm 89

MARK LOVE

Introduction

This sermon proceeded from an assignment to preach on the topic, "The Character of God in the Psalms." Which begs the question, How does one do theology from a hymnal? I am convinced that there is no summary of God's character that could account for every view of God presented in the Psalms. The question is less, What is the character of God in the Psalms? and more What view of God would account for this book of worship?

Given this reframing of the topic, I compared the shape and content of the Psalms to the two hymnals I grew up using in church. The Psalms are more intensely focused on both God and human experience than our hymnals. As Brueggemann points out, the candor of the Psalms regarding the nature of human experience allows God to emerge as the central character of the Psalms. Yet this world of candor would hardly be allowed in most of our churches addicted to the anesthesia of sanitized praise. As Brueggemann suggests, the Psalms are "too abrasive and filled with embarrassing passion" to suit our worship tastes. It was my hope that the sermon could make the case that a recovery of the untamed speech about God we find in Psalms, especially a recovery of lament and complaint language (see John Mark Hicks's essay (chap. 4) in this volume), would allow two prevailing notions of God to guide our worship: God alone is accountable for the world, and God's steadfast love never ceases.

The sermon form intends to let the Psalms perform as a collection. In other words, I want the sermon to account for the fact that the Psalms hold the hallelujahs until the end, after all data about God's participation in the world has been allowed. As a collection, the Psalms move, as Brueggemann suggests, from candor to exuberance. So I frame the sermon imaginatively, asking the listener to attend worship with me in the Psalms. I begin by describing an unidentified worship service so disturbing to me that I walk out in the middle. "I'll never attend church in the Psalms again" reveals that Israel's hymnal is the source of this disturbing worship experience. The sermon ends wistfully, with my wishing I had stayed to the end to join the cascading hallelujahs.

Going to Church in the Psalms

IMPACT, ROCHESTER COLLEGE
OCTOBER 2003

My assignment tonight is "The Character of God in the Psalms." Which is a little like speaking on the subject, "Everything That's Wrong with the Detroit Tigers." Where would you start? Where would you end? Pitching, defense, hitting, minor leagues, coaching? This assignment is daunting.

Still, I'm up to the challenge. Ready? God is Yahweh, El Shaddai, Elohim, a mighty tower, a rock, a fortress. Our God is a stronghold, a sure defense. The Lord of Hosts is a horn of salvation. The Lord is our light, a warrior, a king, a shepherd, a mother, a vinedresser. God is an avenger and a healer. A protector, creator, destroyer. The Lord is lawgiver and judge, a forger of weapons and their destroyer. Our God is a shelter in the storm. God is the storm. God is a place of peace and rest, and God is the disorienting whirlwind. Any questions?

I hope you noticed two things from this quick tour of images of God in the Psalms. The picture we have is rich and diverse. Simply listing images, however, leaves us still a long way from knowing the nature of God in the Psalms. But I also want you to notice that the images are so varied, and sometimes so at odds with one another, that it makes you wonder if the psalmists are speaking of the same God. We have a very difficult task tonight, defining the nature of God in the Psalms.

Let's listen for a more modest point of reference by reading from Psalm 89.

> I will sing of your steadfast love, O LORD, forever;
> with my mouth I will proclaim your faithfulness to all generations.
> I declare that your steadfast love is established forever;
> your faithfulness is as firm as the heavens...
> The heavens are yours, the earth also is yours;
> The world and all that is in it—you have founded them.
> (Ps. 89:1–2, 10)

O, Lord, we seek you through the pages of the Psalms. We trust that in the myriad of images available, you will make yourself known. Amen.

The Strange Church Service

I recently attended an unusual worship service that bothered me to the point that I got up and walked out. Want to hear about it?

The service began as the presider stood and said, "I want to remind you, as we begin our worship today, that we have come to feast on the word of God. If we want to live fruitful lives, if we want to be like trees planted by streams of water,

then we will meditate day and night on the word of the Lord."
And I thought, "That's pretty good." It warmed my Campbellite
heart to begin with an emphasis on the word of God.

Next, the presider said, "I also want to remind you today
that we are a people of prayer. We live our lives unceasingly
before God in prayer. When we lie down at night, we offer our
lives in prayer to God; and as we rise in the morning, we seek
him in prayer. No matter what circumstances we encounter in
life, we are a people who pray." Again, I thought, "Not bad.
Everyone can be reminded that their prayer life is not what it
ought to be, myself included." So far, so good.

But then it got weird. Our presider said, "What should we
pray about today?" A man stood up in the center of the room
(this doesn't happen where I go to church) and said, "I have an
enemy who is out to get me. Now if I'm in the wrong, then I
want God to deal severely with me. But I'm pretty sure my
enemy is the problem. He has treated me unjustly. So I expect
God to deal severely with him, to launch a flaming arrow right
at the guy. Let's pray about that." I thought to myself, "I've
never heard anything like this in church before." But the
congregation, seemingly not fazed at all by this prayer request,
responded, "The steadfast love of the Lord never ceases."

Then another person stood and named his request: "I want
to praise God for His faithfulness today. I was trapped in death's
snare, but God reached out and rescued me, blessed be His
name." And the congregation said, "The steadfast love of the
Lord never ceases." Which was better than the first prayer
request. But how does this guy know that it was God who
rescued him? Before my mind could sort out all the theological
problems with this request, a woman stood and said, "God has
forgotten me. I am in pain day and night and he's hiding from
me. He is ignoring me. I think we ought to pray until we get his
attention." I wondered, "What kind of church have I stumbled
into?" I mean, we pray for healing, but we don't often blame
God for illness or charge him with neglect. But the congregation
responded right on cue, "The steadfast love of the Lord never
ceases."

It went on like this for a while. It had me pining for the
good old days of two songs and a prayer. Get this. At one point

a man stood and said, "I think we should praise God, because after all, who are we that he is mindful of us and yet has made us a little lower than the angels." And immediately this other guy stood up right on top of him and said, "Indeed, who are we that the Lord is mindful of us? He has made us nothing but dust." Now, where I go to church we usually wait until we get to the foyer to have conflict. Not here. Right in the middle of the service they fight about what it means for God to be mindful of humans. Or whether or not God should smite our enemies or turn our weapons into plowshares. And the congregation just keeps responding, "The steadfast love of the Lord never ceases."

Finally, the straw came that broke the camel's back. This young hippie type stood and announced, "I think we need to remind God of what his business is in the world. The poor are being oppressed, and he's doing nothing about it. And the rich are flouting their ill-gotten wealth, mocking God. I think it's time somebody reminded God what his business is in this world." I had had enough! Who talks like this in worship? So, I got up and left. Who is God to these people that they dare to address him like this? I don't think I'll ever worship with the Psalms again.

Two Hymnals: Two Images of God

How does one do theology from a hymnal?

When I was a teenager, I attended the stately old University Church of Christ in Abilene, Texas. We sang hymns each week from "Old Blue." You know "Old Blue"? Otherwise known as *Great Songs of the Church*. Let me say that again with the proper emphasis–*GREAT Songs of the Church*. Average songs need not apply; only the *great* songs of the church are found in this collection. This is not to say that all the songs are equally great. It is still necessary to divide "Old Blue" into gospel songs (which are not quite as lofty in their ambition or accomplishment) and hymns (the highest achievement in songs for worship). The editor provided us a very explicit rationale for the selection of these great songs. The standards followed were truth and soundness, then strength and clarity, poetic beauty and lyric quality: "The music wedded to the words and fit to wing them to the heart." Here's my favorite sentence from the editor's preface: "Resort to common syncopated rhythms or other low unspiritual devices of our day could not be tolerated." We had no unspiritual syncopated rhythms in the University Church of Christ. We sang *great* songs of the church, like so many stained-glass–shape notes in the air. Who is God in these songs? God is high and majestic. The Lord is exalted and lifted up. These songs are not soiled by the common things of life. Instead, they lead us into the rarified air of the presence of God.

But I didn't always attend the University Church of Christ. Other churches I attended had more modest hymnic ambitions. We sang from the hymnal *Songs of the Church*. Not "great songs"– just plain old *Songs of the Church*. This hymnal came in a variety of colors. You could buy green or blue or red or gold. We possessed an assortment of colors, I assume to match our lovely carpet. Nothing fancy about these hymnals.

This songbook specialized in those "low, unspiritual syncopated songs." Every Sunday we sang the Stamps-Baxter tunes–"Where Could I Go But to the Lord?", "The New Song", and "Paradise Valley"–songs that common folk could sing. And we had a common songleader to lead them. He wasn't theologically driven as he picked songs from week to week. His idea of arranging songs around a theme was to choose ones that ended in odd numbers and then to sing only the even verses. Or to choose songs that mentioned human anatomy. So one week we might have songs about feet and hands, the next week, a song about hearts or heads. You get the idea.

And who is God in these songs? Here, we don't have the exalted theology of "Old Blue." In fact, some songs barely refer to God at all… "If the skies above you are gray, you are feeling so blue. If your cares and burdens seem great all the whole day through. There's a silver lining that shines in the heavenly land. Look by faith and see it my friend. Trust in his promises grand. Sing and be happy." Or, "I've got a mansion, just over the hilltop." We sang a lot of songs about heaven that were only peripherally about God. We sang them, not to draw us deeper into life, but to help us forget about our lives and all the trouble we have here on earth. "Farther along we'll know all about it." "Won't it be wonderful there?"

Two very different hymnals. Two very different pictures of God.

God in the Psalms: Viewed from All of Human Life

Who is God in the Psalms—Israel's hymnal? This is a hymnal very different from both "Old Blue" and *Songs of the Church*. Israel's hymnbook is obsessed with God. God is an actor in nearly every Psalm, which makes it very different from *Songs of the Church*. But the Psalms are also nearly equally obsessed with what it is to be human. Common human predicaments and emotions are fully on display in the Psalms, unlike in the very restrained "Old Blue." In fact, it's this second obsession—with what it is to be human—that accounts for the multitude of images of God we listed at the beginning of the sermon.

The Psalms aren't systematic theology. In other words, it's not as if somebody sat down and said, "I want to write a hymn that captures with precision the character of God." These hymns are theology in the moment—God viewed from the human side. God viewed through our joy. God viewed through our grief and sometimes through the disorientation of our despair. These hymns come unvarnished. The psalmists feel no need to cover their words with stained glass. The unrestrained quality of speech in the Psalms produces an impressive variety of images of God, images that sometimes clash with and are hard to reconcile to one another. So the question of God in relation to the Psalms might be, What view of God encourages this kind of diversity? Asked another way, Who is God that he would authorize a hymnal like this?

Let's go back to Psalm 89 and notice verse 11; "The heavens are yours; the earth also is yours. The world and all that is in it—you have founded them." The faith of the psalmist begins with the belief that the only reference point for anything in life is God. Unlike other accounts of reality that depict creation as a struggle between competing gods, the Old Testament declares, "The LORD is our God, the LORD alone" (Deut. 6:4). All things find their source in Yahweh and ultimately serve his purposes in the world. Think of the highest angel, and God is greater. Think of the greatest superpower you can think of, and God is greater. Go to the heights; go to the depths; go to the north; go to the South—God is there and responsible for it all. And here's the point: If God is responsible for it all, if all of life is accountable to God, then all of life is fair game in worship. Both the heights and the depths.

I read today in *The Oakland Press,* your local newspaper, an article on Mother Teresa. Her expressions of faith sound very much like the Psalms. She says, "I am told God lives in me. And yet the reality of darkness and emptiness and coldness is so great that nothing touches my soul." In another diary entry she writes, "I want God, with all the power of my soul, and yet between us there is this terrible separation, heaven from every side is closed." Another entry: "I feel just that terrible pain of loss, of God not wanting me, of God not being, of God not really existing." These words are the kind Israel sets to music and sings in the temple, because Israel is convinced that all of life is connected to God, even the seemingly God-forsaken parts.

If you believe that everything is God's, as Mother Teresa seems to, then you can't take only the good portions of life and say, "this stuff belongs to God, but this stuff over here—the doubt, the pain, the grief—doesn't." If all praise is due God, then so is all complaint, and all grief, and all celebration, and all doubt.

Dangerous and Fully Human in Worship: What Will God Think?

Look, I know that this sounds, well, dangerous. Is this really acceptable speech for worship? After all, our perspectives are so limited. What if we say things in our grief or our failure, or even in our success and joy, that don't correspond with who God really is? What if we cross some kind of line in how we talk about God? What if we're wrong?

Which brings us to another characteristic of God mentioned in Psalm 89: His steadfast love endures forever. God is in this thing for the long haul. Yahweh is not going to abandon the work of redeeming his creation, even if his people don't fully comprehend him. Sometimes we have this image of an easily offended God who is just waiting for an excuse to turn his back on the story. But God is persistently faithful, and not offended by our humanity. God knows that we are finite and limited, and welcomes us into God's presence just as we are. God will not go away! You might, but God won't. The steadfast love of the Lord endures forever!

The Psalms allow God's people to explore the full range of what it means to be human. Our hymnals look so limited in comparison. I notice that we have one of the newer hymnals in the pews tonight. It contains a lot of great songs of praise and quite a few about our heavenly hope. But it offers to God such a limited range of human experience. Where are the laments? The complaints? There is precious little by way of confession. Human experience is expressed only in very generic terms. Where is the grit? the real stuff of life? Too often our hymnals, thin as they are in range of experience, sing too easily of heaven in an effort to take our minds off the very trouble of life that God longs to enter. The Psalms will have none of that.

Sometimes our worship leads me to think we share Homer Simpson's view of God. In one episode of *The Simpsons,* Homer says, "I may not know much about God, but I have to say we've built a really nice cage for Him." Here's the deal. When we limit the range of human expression in our worship, we limit who God can be among us. We build a cage for God with our stained-glass language. When we bring only part of our lives to worship, we limit our awareness of God's involvement in other aspects of life. The paradox of worship, borne out in the Psalms, is that the greater the expression of our humanity, the greater awareness we have of God. The more we confess, the greater the experience of God's mercy. The more vulnerable and helpless we are, the greater God's movement in our midst is perceived. The more limited and finite we are, the greater our appreciation of God. God's steadfast love never ceases.

Staying to the End of Worship

We've got to think long and hard about worship in relation to the Psalms. A greater appreciation for the character of God in the Psalms would demand more honest expression from us in worship. Israel's bold freedom in worship flows from the twin convictions that God is ultimately responsible for all of life and that God's steadfast love endures forever. If we took those notions more seriously, our worship would be changed forever. Our transformed worship would both take our humanity more seriously and allow greater room for an awareness of the almighty God in our lives.

In this way, the Psalms prepare us to receive Christ. Like the Psalms, Jesus holds together both the human and divine. At the cross he holds together a full range of human experience: suffering and joy, life and death, sin and righteousness. All things are being gathered up in Christ for the glory of God. From whom, and through whom, and to whom are all things. Glory be to God in the church! The Psalms prepare us for the encounter with God that is ours in Jesus. And at the cross we say with the congregation gathered in the Psalms, "The steadfast love of the Lord never ceases."

Now, looking back on the day I worshiped with the Psalms, I wish I had stayed to the end. Because this is how worship in the Psalms ends: with cascading hallelujahs. Praise the Lord, praise the Lord, praise the Lord, praise the Lord! Because when all of life can be acknowledged in the presence of God, something wonderful happens: God's people come to know God, and to love God, and to trust God.

It is time to sing the hallelujah (Ps. 150):

Praise the LORD!
Praise God in his sanctuary;
    praise him in his mighty firmament!
Praise him for his mighty deeds;
    praise him according to his surpassing greatness!
Praise him with trumpet sound;
    praise him with lute and harp!
Praise him with tambourine and dance;
    praise him with strings and pipe!
Praise him with clanging cymbals;
    praise him with loud clashing cymbals!
Let everything that breathes praise the LORD!
Praise the LORD!

12

Dust in the Space Between

Psalm 103

JEFF M. CHRISTIAN

Introduction

The following sermon is a limit expression of limit experience. I share Paul Ricoeur's fascination with what can only be known in part, and especially how Walter Brueggemann speaks of the Psalms as inseparable from personal experience in his chapter on the Psalms as "limit expressions." Specifically, Psalm 103 is at once tragic and redemptive. It will not shy away from the pit of life, but neither will it allow a drowning out of its message of redemption. Psalm 103 speaks. If the message is cast in the limit experience of the listener who finds a temporary home in the pit, the message goes on to both declare and embody a word of redemption, a limit expression. It does so by imagining a world where the dust of the pit is exchanged for a crown of compassion. As Brueggemann notes, the realities of guilt and death are met with real resolution by the word of Psalm 103. The guilt of sin is turned into the exuberance of God's mercy extended to God's people.

I understand the thrust of Psalm 103 in the same way J. Clinton McCann Jr. speaks of many of the Psalms: the narrative plot is found in the lives of the listeners. What Paul Scott Wilson calls "fictive plot" in his essay (chap. 6) I tend to incorporate in this sermon vis-à-vis the possibility of the listener's objections based on his or her own experience in life, namely, that sin gets in the way of the good news of God's grace. This sermon takes the time to "mumble about reality" in order to highlight God's redeeming righteousness all the more. In bending the details of the text to our experience, the following sermon seeks to preach Psalm 103 in such a way that sounds as though the listener wrote the Psalm by his or her own hand. We all sin. The world falls short of God's glory. But the Lord works righteousness and justice for all the oppressed.

Dust in the Space Between

GLENWOOD CHURCH OF CHRIST—TYLER, TEXAS
MAY, 2004

Sin is patient. Sin strolls around in broad daylight and waits for us in the dark. Sin is noise that moves in and out of our lives at random, at a moment deafening. Even so, God assures us He is present. God's voice follows in the coming moments, a voice filled with grace where you find yourself immersed in silence. The sound of sin is silenced, and then the silence is broken by a motherly voice. The whisper says my transgressions have been removed.

But as difficult as it is to admit, we are not ready to believe. Not yet.

The words of the tender voice get bogged down almost immediately. The renewal of "forgive" and "heal" is covered by the oil slick of "disease" and "pit."

Psalm 103 pictures an ideal world in which oppression is sheltered by the righteousness and justice of the Lord. Those in the pit are pulled out by their dirty necks, and God covers their mussed up hair with crowns of love and compassion.

But all is not well, because those with ears to hear this ancient song know the tune better than they would care to know. Those with ears to hear Psalm 103 have ears filled with pain. They do not want the wisdom that comes from experience. Keep it; it's yours. Given the chance, they would exchange the cave for sunshine. The only reason verse 4 brings joy to the listener where "God redeems your life from the pit" is because the listener knows what a pit looks like from the inside. You as the listener know the depth of the pit, how wide it is, and how damp it smells. God may be slow to anger, but my experience in this hole makes me wonder. When we finally make it out of the pit, the wind buffets us so badly that we wonder whether or not we should return to the comfort of sin. Egypt was not that bad. Sure God made His ways known to Moses. But will God do the same for us? How can God be heard when sin uses a bullhorn?

Sin is mean. Sin is crafty. Sin is patient. The noise of sin refuses to be ignored, deafening the attention of its prey, interrupting them with the strange allure of phrases that sound almost truthful, everything from short sentences such as "What if…" and "Come on, it's not that bad" to sell-out sermons concerned more with maintaining the status quo.

But God still speaks. God fills the mouths of those who preach and those who live, helping us to imagine a world where God's love is like a child who spreads his arms as far as he can stretch to shout, "I love you this much!" Psalm 103 asks the noise to settle down, slowly, as if the noise knows it needs to hear something it does not know. The tender voice of the poet speaks: "As far as the east is from the west, so far has he removed our transgressions from us" (v. 12).

Really?

If We Are Honest, We Cannot Help but Wonder

When we grab our remote controls for the evening news, sit down in our easy chairs ,and turn on the world, we do not see the distance between the two points of east and west. All we can see is the space between. The news shapes a story every day, an ongoing drama in which people hone the trade of reporting transgressions. The evening news is good at being bad. It reminds us in an almost godly way that we are dust. So we turn off the broadcast and return to the pit. The pit is familiar. It feels like a shelter. Our pride is welcomed there in all of its forms. The grace up on the surface is hard to understand.

Soldiers were killed today in a far-away place. Shouldn't we resign ourselves to expect that? How could we possibly shoulder the naivete that would dare to pray for peace in a world that sounds like this?

Did you hear that Jim and Marie are getting divorced?

There was a ten-car pileup on I-20 this morning.

Children were taken hostage yesterday in Southern Russia.

How should we confront Glenn with his drinking problem?

The church parking lot is filled with trophies of greed.

Timmy's teacher caught him in another lie at school.

Warlords in Somalia have the whole country held hostage.

Egypt wasn't that bad. At least it was familiar. The only problem with being lifted out of the pit is that the surface feels like a forty-year desert where peace avoids me and where sin taunts me from the sidelines. Oppression takes place on the surface, too, you know. Is it any wonder that one of the earliest Christian sermons tells a church teetering on the edge of the pit to strengthen their drooping arms and their weak knees (Heb. 12:12)? God gives us ears to hear a story of youthful vitality only because we are old.

The odd thing about Psalm 103 is that we need to hear its message whether we are in the pit or on the surface, for it all makes up the landscape of the space between. The message dares us to speak, whether those around us call it wise or naïve. The message we are to speak is whispered in our ears: "Praise the LORD, O my soul" (v. 1, NIV). Then it is shouted from the rooftops: Praise the LORD, O my soul! Whether on top of the mountain or deep in the valley, my message is made clear: Praise the LORD, O my soul.

We praise, not because of what God will do, but because of what God does. God forgives. God heals. God meets lepers and tells them they can walk through the marketplace for the first time. God empties the pit of the guilty and meets them with crowns, robes, and a fatted calf. The Lord works righteousness and justice for all of the oppressed. God makes divine deeds known to God's people. God takes our sin as it laps against the shores of the Atlantic coast, strips it from our clutches, and dumps it in the Pacific.

When we grab the remote control to turn on the news, we are reminded of the space between where those of us reside who are made of dust, those of us who long to hear a message beyond even the surface of the pit. Perhaps the news needs a prophet at the end of the broadcast, not one who will share a human interest story or a cute illustration. The end of the newscast—and the end of the sermon for that matter—needs a prophet who will dare to imagine a God who redeems people from the headlines, a God who invades the noisy space between to tell us that God resides there as well. And because we reside, sometimes in the pit and sometimes on the surface, whatever our lot, our message is the same: Praise the LORD, O my soul.

The greatest thing about Psalm 103 is the way it abandons its original metaphor. Realizing that the space between east and west is not an apt description of God's love, the poet abandons images of space and time in verse 17 in exchange for an immeasurable description, words that would go well at the end of the broadcast.

From Everlasting to Everlasting

God moves among people to create a new world. God encourages people to say that God's ways are mysterious and helps them to realize that the most mysterious activity of God is grace. God speaks a world into existence where sin is trampled underfoot, where the house of cards built on the table of my pride is shaken, and then shaken some more. The world will revolve without my input. But without God's benefits, it will stop. The wisdom of Psalm 103 replaces my need for acceptance with God's compassion, a compassion God pours over God's children, the listeners of this Psalm.

God Distances Our Sin from Us

God takes the young mother whose temper is winning the battle and reminds her that God is able to renew her youth. God speaks a Word to the nations to call their greed into question. God reminds the boss what it was like to be the employee. God gives us health where there is disease, grace where there is resentment, satisfaction where there is apprehension, and peace where there is noise. God settles the dust and invites us to join the end of Psalm 103, where angels praise the Lord, where the heavenly host leads true worship, where rocks and trees cry the name of God, and where those with ears to hear are lifted from the pit.

O my soul.

13

Sing to the Lord a New Song?

Trouble Leaving the Lament:
Psalm 146

DAVID FLEER

Introduction

Ron Cox observes that the early Christian application of the lament to the life of Jesus "unduly circumscribed" the emotional honesty of the genre.[1] The lament, as Hicks reminds us,[2] is an act of faith, an appeal to divine faithfulness that assumes hope. Now that we are learning to linger in personal and communal lament, too quick a departure for recovery truncates legitimate emotion articulated in the Psalter and appropriated by the congregation. Thus, when the following sermon lingers in lament, it recognizes the legitimacy of the experience.

This sermon follows Walter Brueggemann's categorization of the Psalms as Orientation, Disorientation, and New Orientation[3] and attempts to prevent "New Orientation" from moving us into a limit expression that "buttons down everything."[4] New Orientation should not restrict us to a safe middle ground that cuts off the extremities of our life. Psalm 146 avoids this restriction by repositioning us in the "thick communal memory" of God acting in justice.[5] The sermon at first hesitates accepting the Psalm as a script to be read and eschews the disposition of Psalm 146 that begins and ends with praise. Instead, the sermon moves to praise only after it has overcome suspicion at the cheerfulness of the Psalm's first words and lived in the Psalm's middle section, where a full-bodied remembrance brings to life God's acts of justice on behalf of the hopeless. Hearers are prepared for a "New Orientation," a move out toward praise, when they find themselves in step with the psalmist, allowing memory to create hope and descriptive agony to evolve into doxology.

The sermon was delivered during the concluding worship at the Rochester College Sermon Seminar, May 2004, where the congregation was a collection of preachers who for forty-eight hours had studied and reflected on the Psalms, lament, and preaching. The sermon's personal reference to our son Luke, whom many in the audience knew and for whom they had prayed in prior weeks, reflects the concrete nature of the sermon and the ethos of the preacher. We are grateful that at the time of this writing Luke's progress is beyond our early expectations.

Sing to the Lord a New Song?

ROCHESTER COLLEGE SERMON SEMINAR
MAY 26, 2004

Trouble Leaving the Lament

It seems pretty simple: Psalm 146, a psalm of New Orientation. A fitting conclusion to the Psalter, this final doxology, this Hallelujah section. And Psalm 146 is an appropriate conclusion to this volume.

It seems pretty simple, this speaker who begins by affirming his determination to offer God his lifelong praise. This bold contrast between the Lord who performs and the princes of this earth "whose dreams die with them" (v. 4, author's paraphrase). It seems pretty simple to sing to the Lord this new song.

The Psalms are neatly grouped as psalms of Orientation, Disorientation, and New Orientation. Orientation: you reap what you sow. What our coaches and parents and teachers taught us. Work hard; get a good education; and you'll be a minister one day. And from those promoting continuing education, attend this seminar, and you'll be an excellent preacher one day. Psalms of Orientation, such as Psalm 90 and Psalm 1. Life is livable. The world is a reliable place. We awake from a night's sleep and sort out our dreams and dismiss our nightmares and get on with the pleasant chores of life. Psalms of Orientation.

Then we meet Psalms of Disorientation. Israel, our model, didn't hesitate to give full voice to fear and anger and dismay. God can be unpredictable. And so, the laments. And so Job 3, which follows Job's first disaster, after which the narrator says, "In all this Job did not sin" (Job 1:22). Which is followed by the second disaster, after which the narrator says, "In all this Job did not sin with his lips" (2:10). Which is followed by a week's worth of contemplation, after which the narrator says, "Job opened his mouth and cursed the day of his birth" (3:1). Which, for recovering Fundamentalists, feels good to be so honest. I wish I'd never been born. I'd rather be in the grave than living in these troubles.

It wears a friendship thin, pushes the "statute of limitations" on sympathy. Causes friends to cross and recross the street to avoid hearing your honest response to their greeting, "So, how's it goin'?" and pushes Eliphaz, Bildad, and Zophar to remedial preaching, with us as their audience.

But the Psalms of Disorientation are still true. These Psalms of lament, Job's lament, where birth is sometimes a tragedy and death is sometimes a welcome relief–these deep laments are true.

And then there are the Psalms of New Orientation that celebrate a new world, that celebrate the Lord's generosity, that say, "Sing unto the Lord a new song."

It all seems so simple and straightforward that Psalm 146 almost reads like a script.

"Here you go. Read this."
"But, but…"
"No, go ahead and just read it."
"I may not be ready to read it."

One minister advises people who come to him asking where to begin reading scripture. He tells them, "Just open the Psalms to any page and begin reading. Sooner or later you will find something that speaks to your situation; you'll find something that seems to be speaking directly to you.

But, someone says, "It's not that easy." Someone else says, "It's not that simple."

The movement from Disorientation to New Orientation isn't easy when you've really had your life turned around. The happy psalmist of 146 can look like the young man who straps the bungee cord on your ankles and calves and asks you to jump.

"Wait, wait," you say. "Let's think about this. Give me time. I may change my mind. I may not jump. I think I'll stay here and let you jump to the *next level.*"

Disorientation alone can stall our souls.

We have a friend who talks about his life "B.C." Before cancer. "Our lives started when our daughter was diagnosed with brain cancer two years ago. Since then, life has been so focused on her pain and recovery and struggle that I don't remember life B.C."

And we're going to hand our friend Psalm 146, this psalm of New Orientation?

The truth is that Disorientation stalls our souls. It is not easy to move into this "new song."

Many of you have been aware of the events that took place in our lives three months ago. On Wednesday evening, February 4, just after we'd fallen asleep, the phone rang, and our reality changed. The message began, "Hello Fleer family, this is Rene Anderson with Oxford Emergency Medical. Luke has been in an accident here on the Lapeer Highway. His vital signs look very good. He is talking to us."

She had a cheery sound to her voice. I wondered if this was her natural tone or if she was purposely communicating some kind of hope.

"The Oxford Firefighters used the jaws of life to extricate him from the vehicle, and he is about to be life flighted to Royal Oak Beaumont," she said. "They have an excellent trauma team."

It is the kind of news that makes the listening parent inhale and inhale and inhale, thinking that maybe the oxygen will clear up the fog. But it doesn't alter anything.

"He's coherent," she said. "His vital signs look good."

Harm done to a child is qualitatively different from economic concerns, home ownership woes, work frustration, and mid-life crises. Even so, Disorientation calls the soul to linger.

The same minister who advised, "Just open the Psalms and begin reading," thought the Psalms had great insight into the human condition.

He said, "I once advised a woman about to undergo surgery for cancer to read the Psalms straight through, preferably in the King James Version. I wanted her to read the whole thing in one or two sittings in order to have an immersion experience into the soul of the writer."

"She did as I suggested," the minister reported, "and when I asked her how it went, she replied that she had had no idea that the psalmist knew who she was, her precise condition, and what she needed and when."

More helpful is the woman's response, "When the psalmist rejoiced, so did I. When the psalmist howled and cried, so did I."

The preacher sent her into scripture with an agenda, what she needed. But she was nourished when she fell into step with the psalmist: "When the psalmist rejoiced, I rejoiced; when the psalmist howled and cried, so did I."

When two cars, both traveling fifty-five miles per hour, collide head on, firefighters approach the wreck expecting fatalities. We witnessed our son endure four surgeries on his broken pelvis, crushed fibula, damaged knee, muscle and nerve loss, unbearable pain, compromised life, and threatened mobility at age twenty-three. It was a nightmare that didn't clear up in the morning.

This Psalm of New Orientation is hard to read when you are moving out of Disorientation. You approach a Psalm like this with great caution, sniff around it, a little suspicious. Especially the verses that sound so cheery, "Praise the LORD! Praise the LORD, O my soul! I will praise the LORD as long as I live; I will sing praises to my God all my life long" (146:1–2). They have a purple hue, a Barney-like sound to them. "I love God; God loves me; we're a happy fam-i-lee." Praise and worship gruel that has chased off the meaningful hymns. Like this medley: "Beautiful, beautiful, Jesus is beautiful…you are more beautiful than diamonds…I keep falling in love with him over and over again, over and over again…you are beautiful beyond description, your face is all I seek…you're so easy to adore, I just want to be, I just want to be, I just want to be, I just want to be with you."

We want to say, "no kissing please." After Disorientation, we grow suspicious of such medleys.

Psalm 146 is still a hard Psalm to read, especially when read as a contrast between God and human beings.[6] Frankly, human beings have been pretty good. From the Oxford firefighters to the surgeons, nurses, and the trauma team at Royal Oak Beaumont to Luke's preacher, who visited more than a dozen times, and the woman who decorated his hospital room, the prayers, meals, and cards from Christians and non-Christians alike. Good hearts, kind spirits, concerned people.

Oh, an occasional Bildad would wander by, announcing traditional piety, saying, "You all will be better persons for this." Or, "It could be worse." Offensive, but harmless.

The ones who had it worse—whose twenty-three–year-old son had died in a car wreck—understood best and held us and cried with us.

A Sunday school student from Ohio wrote Luke, "I hope you are better soon and even if you don't, people will still love you even though you may not look the same. You don't have to look the same on the outside but you still look the same on the inside. God be with you while you heel." That's spelled h-e-e-l.

It wasn't people with whom I had a quarrel. My quarrel was with God. It wasn't, "Why me? or Why us? or Why our son?" But, "Why is it like *this*? Good people doing good deeds, getting crushed? *Why?*"

I'm not asking how does the bumble bee fly, or how was the Grand Canyon formed. But, how can God allow this? Does God care? Is God involved? Just when should we expect God back from break? These are not questions; these are penetrating concerns, essential expressions of our existence. Why?

I'd walk away from this text. How many times have we read or heard Will Willimon say, in his Carolina drawl, "I didn't pick this text. I'd never choose this passage. This text chose me."

Well, I did pick this text, assigned it and accepted it…last July. And then came February and March. Otherwise, I'd turn the page back to a lament. But like a script, it's handed to me for us to read and for us to live.

So, I read this script to you. I've gained courage to stay with it from Luke himself, who says that he hasn't questioned God. He says, "I can't believe I'm alive." He says that God was with him there, present, holding him together the moment the two cars collided. He encourages me to stay with the script. And all the people who were so kind—where did they come from?

But why the cheery words to open this Psalm? I don't know. Maybe the psalmist is trying to carry us in.

And look at this. God isn't contrasted with human beings. God is contrasted with princes, overlords, power brokers, insurance companies, hospital bureaucracies.

Move in deeper, and feel the magnetic pull of this Re-orienting psalm. It draws us in as it appeals to our memory.[7]

Stand with me on the banks of the Columbia River. Face south; look toward Portland; and listen to the names of the hospitals: St. Joseph's, Adventist, Providence, Good Samaritan. Do you recognize these original names? The people who founded these hospitals were following the God of New Orientation. Now look at the effects.

Let's visit Atlanta and Montgomery and Selma, the essential venues of the civil rights movement. Where are we? Why, we are in churches, Ebenezer and Dexter Avenue. Look at the black-and-white photograph on the wall. You recognize the leaders at the bottom of the picture: the Reverend Ralph Abernathy, the Reverend Martin Luther King Jr. Do you see the other clergy around them? Who are the mass of people marching with them? They are people of God, "execut[ing] justice for the oppressed" (Ps. 146:7).

Another person was drawn to this text. His inaugural address was from a passage very similar to Psalm 146. He said, "Release to the captives, recovery of sight to the blind, freedom for the downtrodden. That's me." (Compare Lk. 4:18.) And when John the Baptist, in prison, wondered if Jesus was the Messiah, Jesus said, "Tell John that in my ministry the blind see, the lame walk, lepers are cleansed and the poor have the Gospel preached to them." (See Lk. 7:22.) New Orientation says, "Remember that God 'executes justice for the oppressed, gives food to the hungry and sets the prisoner free.'" (See Ps. 146:7.)

Remember Jesus' ministry, and allow yourself to be pulled into this psalm of New Orientation.

Did you know that the Psalms were the prayer book Jesus knew? You knew that didn't you. But did you know that for years this Psalm was part of the Christian's daily morning prayer? They knew that this Psalm expresses a faith in God, an awareness of a new responsibility for fellow human beings. Which is a terrible gift–to have experienced the tender mercies of God and to show God's tender mercies to others.

Life can be ruthless. Experience can be harsh. And we find ourselves hopeless against the forces, no longer masters of our worlds.

Read the Psalms, the minister said. Yes, read the Psalms of New Orientation, you who have been in lament. Read this Psalm in step, as a script. Read it from the middle out, and train your eyes on the memory of God's righteous deeds. Train your eyes on the hospitals and movements of justice and especially on Jesus, from his inaugural sermon to every event in his ministry. And what are you looking at? You are looking into the character of God. And what do you see? You are seeing the radical, transforming power of God. You see a power at work on behalf of the weak and the innocent.

So work out to the beginning of this passage with the memory of justice. That God is reliable. That God holds it together. Work it out to say that we confess that life is a gift, that we wish to be used in God's cause. That we yield ourselves to God and God's community. We will praise the Lord as long as we live; we will sing praises to our God all our life long.

So take this script home with you to pray and preach and live as God uses you to help form the character of God's people into a Christian community.

Notes

Introduction: Performing the Psalms and the World Imagined in the Psalter

[1]See later in this book, Walter Brueggemann's "Psalms in Narrative Performance."

[2]Garrett Green, *Imagining God: Theology and the Religious Imagination* (Grand Rapids: Eerdmans, 1989), 134.

[3]This is the question set out by Luke Timothy Johnson. Among Johnson's many volumes the reader may wish to consider an instance where Johnson applies his project on Hebrews to the task of preaching. See Luke Timothy Johnson, "Hebrews' Challenge to Christians: Christology and Discipleship," in *Preaching Hebrews,* ed. David Fleer and Dave Bland (Abilene, Tex.: Abilene Christian University Press, 2003), 11–28 and David Fleer, "Preaching and the World Hebrews Imagines," in *Preaching Hebrews,* 1–8.

[4]Will Willimon and other postliberals are asking these same fundamental questions. See David Fleer and Dave Bland, "The World Imagined by the Eighth Century Prophets: Moving Toward a New Preaching Paradigm" in *Preaching the Eighth Century Prophets,* ed. David Fleer and Dave Bland (Abilene, Tex.: Abilene Christian University Press, 2004), 1–7.

[5]For examples of application, see Mark Love's re-performance of Psalm 46 (chap. 9) in the light of Brueggemann's suggestions in the first chapter and David Fleer's sermon collated under Brueggemann's advice (chap. 13, on Psalm 146). Two sermons (chaps. 10 and 12) develop texts explored in the first section (Psalm 73; 103).

[6]For his survey Wilson selected McCann before he knew of McCann's participation in the Sermon Seminar and this volume. The reader should note points of contrast from Wilson's assessment of McCann's audience-centered approach in his earlier work against the theological origins of the essay in this volume.

[7]Wilson is following Walter Brueggemann's suggestion elsewhere that, "almost no one assumes that the Psalms are 'records' of what happened. They are rather, as all historical remembering is, rhetorical acts which shape the past in certain ways...never innocent or neutral." Brueggemann, *Abiding Astonishment: Psalms, Modernity, and the Making of History* (Louisville: Westminster/John Knox Press, 1991), 13.

[8]"The Psalms as Limit Expressions." Page 41 mentions the prison scandal.

[9]Mark Love, "Though Mountains Shake in the Sea," p. 141 of this volume.

Chapter 1: Psalms in Narrative Performance

[1]See Walter Brueggemann, "Voice as Counter to Violence," *Calvin Theological Journal* 36 (2001): 22–33.

[2]On the dramatic case of the way in which "silence" served the Nazi Holocaust, see Peter Haidu, "The Dialectics of Unspeakability: Language, Silence, and the Narratives of Desubjectification," in *Probing the Limits of Representation: Nazism and the "Final Solution,"* ed. Saul Friedlander (Cambridge: Harvard University Press, 1992), 277–99. The sense of the "totalism" of the Holocaust has been well articulated by Zygmunt Bauman, *Modernity and Holocaust* (Cambridge: Polity Press, 1991).

[3]See Alice Miller, *Thou Shalt Not Be Aware: Society's Betrayal of the Child,* trans. Hildegarde and Hunter Hannum (New York: Farrar, Straus and Giroux, 1984).

⁴See Jacques Ellul, *The Humiliation of the Word* (Grand Rapids, Mich.: Eerdmans, 1988); *The Technological Society* (London: Jonathan Cape, 1965).

⁵See Walter Brueggemann, *Abiding Astonishment: Psalms, Modernity, and the Making of History,* Literary Currents in Biblical Interpretation (Louisville: Westminster John Knox Press, 1991); Gerhard von Rad, *The Problem of the Hexateuch and Other Essays* (New York: McGraw-Hill, 1966), 11–12 and passim.

⁶See Amos N. Wilder, "Story and Story-World," *Interpretation* 37 (1983): 353–64.

⁷See Walter Brueggemann, "From Hurt to Joy, From Death to Life," *Interpretation* 28 (1974): 3–19.

⁸Claus Westermann, *The Psalms: Structure, Content & Message* (Minneapolis: Augsburg, 1980), 73–83.

⁹On this structure in the Exodus narrative, see James Plastaras, *The God of Exodus* (Milwaukee: The Bruce Publishing Company, 1966).

¹⁰Brevard S. Childs, "Psalm Titles and Midrashic Exegesis," *Journal of Semitic Studies* 16 (1971): 137–50.

¹¹On the acceptance of individual speech as the speech of the community, see Thomas F. Green, *Voices: The Educational Formation of Conscience* (Notre Dame: University of Notre Dame Press, 1999), 148–67.

Chapter 2: The Psalms as Limit Expressions

¹Erhard Gerstenberger, "Psalms," *Old Testament Form Criticism,* ed. by John H. Hayes (San Antonio, Tx.: Trinity University Press, 1974), 179–223; *Psalms Part 1 with an Introduction to Cultic Poetry,* The Forms of the Old Testament Literature 14 (Grand Rapids, Mich.: Eerdmans, 1988).

²Because praise is linked to material reality, it is possible to do a rough "sociology of praise." Thus, African American Baptists sing hymns loudly and vigorously; white Methodists still sound out in ways that would please Wesley; Presbyterians tend to mumble; and Episcopalians hire people to sing for them!

³Paul Ricoeur, "Biblical Hermeneutics," *Semeia* 4 (1975): 107–45.

⁴Paul Ricoeur, *Essays on Biblical Interpretation* (Philadelphia: Fortress Press, 1980), 75–90.

⁵Ricoeur, "Biblical Hermeneutics," 138.

⁶Ricoeur's entire program of imagination is an attempt to keep truth open in a way that resists fixity, for which idolatry is the theological expression.

⁷Ricoeur, "Biblical Hermeneutics," 114–22.

⁸See the notion of the "classic" by David Tracy, *The Analogical Imagination: Christian Theology and the Culture of Pluralism* (New York: Crossroad, 1981).

⁹See Denise Levertov, *The Poet in the World* (New York: New Directions Books, 1973), 49 and passim.

¹⁰Emmanuel Levinas, *Totality and Infinity: An Essay on Exteriority* (Pittsburgh: Duquesne University Press, 1969).

¹¹See Clint McCann's example of the "theology of the market" (chap. 3). Or, as we say in my tradition, "You can critique the Bible, but you cannot critique the *Wall Street Journal.*"

¹²Ron Suskind, *The Price of Loyalty: George W. Bush, The White House, and the Education of Paul O'Neill* (New York: Simon & Schuster, 2004), 292.

¹³Alvin W. Gouldner, *The Coming Crisis of Western Sociology* (New York: Basic Books, 1970); Jacques Ellul, *The Technological Society* (New York: Alfred Knopf, 1965).

¹⁴Hans Georg Gadamer, *Truth and Method* (New York: Seabury Press, 1975).

¹⁵Here, I deliberately refer to the totalism of Levinas. The root term, of course, relates to totalitarianism, a practice to which the market economy is prone.

¹⁶See David Blumenthal, *Facing the Abusive God: A Theology of Protest* (Louisville: Westminster John Knox Press, 1993).

[17]Tania Oldenhage, *Parables For Our Time* (Oxford: Oxford University Press, 2002), chapter 11.

[18]Terrence Des Pres, *The Survivor: An Anatomy of Life in the Death Camps* (New York: Pocket Books, 1977).

[19]On this Psalm, see Walter Brueggemann, *The Psalms and the Life of Faith* (Minneapolis: Fortress Press, 1995), 258–67.

[20]See the summary of Brevard S. Childs, *Introduction to the Old Testament as Scripture* (Philadelphia: Fortress Press, 1979), 517–18.

[21]On the Oracles Against the Nations, see Norman K. Gottwald, *All the Kingdoms of the Earth: Israelite Prophecy and International Relations in the Ancient Near East* (New York: Harper and Row, 1964); and briefly, Walter Brueggemann, "Patriotism for Citizens of the Penultimate Superpower," *Dialog* 42 (Winter 2003): 336–43.

Chapter 3: Greed, Grace, and Gratitude

[1]For a fuller description and an exact quote of Tracy, see Eugene Kennedy, "A Dissenting Voice: Catholic Theologian David Tracy," *New York Times Magazine,* (9 November 1986), 25.

[2]The song is on the compact disc entitled "*Twenty-five*" (Rykodisc, 1998). Words and music are by Bernice Johnson Reagon.

[3]See *Guatemala, Never Again! Recovery of Historical Memory Project: The Official Report of the Human Rights Office, Archdiocese of Guatemala* (Maryknoll, N.Y.: Orbis Books, 1999). Jose Antonio Puac is listed on page ii as one of the "Diocesan Coordinators."

[4]J. V. Kinnier Wilson, "Mental Diseases of Ancient Mesopotamia," in *Diseases in Antiquity: A Survey of Diseases, Injuries, and Surgery of Early Populations,* ed. Don Brothwell and A. T. Sandison (Springfield, Ill.: Charles C. Thomas, 1967), 371.

[5]Reinhold Niebuhr, *Leaves from the Notebook of a Tamed Cynic* (Chicago, New York: Willett, Clark & Colby, 1929; San Francisco: Harper and Row, 1980), 140 (page citation is to the reprint).

[6]Ibid.

[7]Marcus Borg, "Re-Visioning Christianity: The Christian Life," transcript from the 2000 TCPC Forum. Information accessed at www.tcpc.org/resources/articles/revisioning_christianity.htm on December 28, 2004.

[8]Roland E. Murphy, *Experiencing Our Biblical Heritage* (Peabody, Mass.: Hendrickson, 2001), 121.

[9]James L. Mays, *The Lord Reigns: A Theological Handbook to the Psalms* (Louisville: Westminster John Knox Press, 1994), 37.

[10]Douglas John Hall, "On Being the Church after Christendom," in *In Essentials Unity: Reflections on the Nature and Purpose of the Church, in Honor of Frederick R. Trost,* ed. M. Douglas Meeks and Robert Mutton (Minneapolis: Kirk House, 2001), 46.

[11]Martin Luther King Jr. *A Testament of Hope: The Essential Writings and Speeches of Martin Luther King Jr.,* ed. James M. Washington (San Francisco: HarperSanFranciso, 1986), 89.

[12]Joseph Stiglitz, *Globalization and Its Discontents* (New York: Norton, 2002), 20.

[13]Ibid., 220–21, 230; emphasis added with the exception of the word *almost.*

[14]Ibid., 252.

[15]For a helpful perspective along these line, see Deirdre McCloskey, "Capital Gains: How Economic Growth Benefits the World," *The Christian Century* 121, no. 9, (May 4, 2004): 24–30 (excerpted from her essay "Avarice, Prudence, and the Bourgeois Virtues," in *Having: Property and Possessions in Religious and Social Life,* ed. William Schweiker and Charles Matthewes [Grand Rapids, Mich.: Eerdmans, 2004]).

[16]Presentation by Victorio Araya at the Latin American Biblical University, San Jose, Costa Rica, January 22, 2003.

[17]Cited in Phyllis Tickle, *Greed: The Seven Deadly Sins* (Oxford/New York: Oxford University Press, 2004), 18.

¹⁸See Leslie Scanlon, "Enough Is Best in a Time of Plenty," *The Presbyterian Outlook* 186, no. 5 (February 9, 2004): 5.

¹⁹Brian D. McLaren, *A New Kind of Christian: A Tale of Two Friends on a Spiritual Journey* (San Francisco: Jossey-Bass, 2001), 112–13.

²⁰See Mary Jo Leddy, *Radical Gratitude* (Maryknoll, N.Y.: Orbis Books, 2002), especially chap. 2, "Perpetual Dissatisfaction," 14–37.

²¹Mary Pipher, *The Shelter of Each Other: Rebuilding Our Families* (New York: Ballantine, 1996), 26, 94.

²²Singer-songwriter David Wilcox effectively captures and communicates this danger in two of his songs, "Never Enough" on a compact disc entitled *Underneath* (Vanguard Records, 1999), and "Advertising Man" on a compact disc entitled *Home Again* (A&M Records, 1991).

²³James M. Childs, *Greed: Economics and Ethics in Conflict* (Minneapolis: Fortress Press, 2000), 6.

²⁴Leddy, *Radical Gratitude;* see especially chap. 3, 38–70.

²⁵On the importance of the theme of "refuge" in the Psalter, see Jerome F. D. Creach, *Yahweh as Refuge and the Editing of the Hebrew Psalter,* JSOTSup 217 (Sheffield: Sheffield Academic Press, 1996).

²⁶Elsa Tamez, *The Amnesty of Grace: Justification by Faith from a Latin American Perspective,* trans. Sharon H. Ringe (Nashville: Abingdon Press, 1993), esp. 134–40.

²⁷James C. Edwards, *The Plain Sense of Things: The Fate of Religion in an Age of Normal Nihilism* (University Park, Pa.: Penn State University Press, 1997), 53, 56, 57.

²⁸Walter Brueggemann, "Bounded by Obedience and Praise: The Psalms as Canon," *Journal for the Study of the Old Testament* 50 (1991): 67.

Chapter 4: Preaching Community Laments

¹Lament was private and personal, though there were some significant exceptions. For a notable instance, consider the Challenger accident in 1986.

²Retrieved from http://www.negrospirituals.com/news-song/sometimes_i_ fell.htm on March 16, 2005.

³Retrieved from http://www.negrospirituals.com/news-song/trouble_done_ bore_me_down.htm on March 16, 2005.

⁴Judg. 20:26; Joel 2:15; Jer. 36:9; 2 Chr. 20:3; Esth. 4:3, 16.

⁵Judg. 20:26; 1 Sam. 7:5; Joel 1:14; Jer. 36:6, 9; 2 Chr. 20:4, 13; Esth. 4:16.

⁶Judg. 20:26; 1 Sam. 7:6; Isa. 22:12; Jer. 14:12.

⁷Isa. 22:12; Isa. 58:5; Jer. 6:26; Esth. 4:3.

⁸Judg. 20:23, 26.

⁹Josh. 7:6–9; 1 Sam. 7:5; 2 Kings 19:14–15; 2 Chr. 20:5; Joel 2:17. Cf. Paul Wayne Ferris Jr., *The Genre of Communal Lament in the Bible and the Ancient Near East,* SBL Dissertation Series 127 (Atlanta: Scholars Press, 1992), 107–8.

¹⁰Walter C. Bouzard, *We Have Heard With Our Ears, O God: Sources of the Communal Laments in the Psalms,* SBL Dissertation Series 159 (Atlanta: Scholars Press, 1997), 211–12.

¹¹Ferris, *Lament,* 14, identifies the following Psalms as communal laments in his study of the genre: Psalms 31, 35, 42–44, 56, 59–60, 69, 74, 77, 79–80, 83, 85, 89, 94, 102, 109, 137, and 142. B. W. Anderson, *Out of the Depths* (Philadelphia: Westminster Press, 1983), 242, considers Psalms 12, 14, 58, 60, 74, 79–80, 83, 85, 90, 94, 123, 126, and 129 as communal laments. W. H. Bellinger Jr., *Psalms: Reading and Studying the Book of Psalms* (Peabody, Mass.: Hendrickson, 1990), 45, also adds Psalms 44, 53, 106, and 108. Bouzard, *We Have Heard,* 113, notes that everyone recognizes Psalms 44, 60, 74, 79–80, 83, 85, and 89 as clear expressions of this genre.

¹²Ferris, *Lament,* 89–100. The categories are Ferris's, whereas the descriptions are mine based on his discussion.

¹³Ibid., 92.

[14]Based on Loren D. Crow, "The Rhetoric of Psalm 44," *Zeitschrift für die altestamentliche Wissenschaft* 104 (1992): 394–401; and Ingvar Floysvik, *When God Becomes My Enemy: The Theology of the Complaint Psalms* (St. Louis: Concordia, 1997), 59.

[15]Crow, "Rhetoric," 397.

[16]David R. Blumenthal, *Facing the Abusing God: A Theology of Protest* (Louisville: Westminster John Knox Press, 1993), 99–100; information obtained from http://www.emory.edu/UDR/BLUMENTHAL/MidrashPs44.html on December 31, 2004.

[17]Hans-Jocahim Kraus, *Psalms 60–150* (Minneapolis: Augsburg, 1989); and Marvin E. Tate, *Psalms 51–100*, WBC 20 (Dallas: Word, 1990), both quoting Jeremias.

[18]James L. Mays, *Psalms,* Interpretation (Louisville: Westminster John Knox Press, 1994), 211.

[19]Augustine, *Psalm 58.1,* obtained fromhttp://www.ccel.org/fathers2/NPNF1–08/npnf1–08–65.htm#P1565_1174137 on December 31, 2004.

[20]Erich Zengar, *A God of Vengeance? Understanding the Psalms of Divine Wrath,* trans. Linda M. Maloney (Louisville: Westminster John Knox Press, 1996), 38.

[21]Dietrich Bonhoeffer, "A Bonhoeffer Sermon," trans. Donald Bloesch, *Theology Today* 38, no. 4 (January 1982): 465–71, obtained from http://theologytoday.ptsem.edu/jan1982/v38-4-article3.htm on December 31, 2004.

[22]See the homily on Psalm 58 by Mitri Raheb, a Palestinian Arab Christian minister in Israel, at http://www.pcusa.org/peacemaking/conferences/2003/psalmsermon.htm, obtained December 31, 2004.

[23]Bonhoeffer, "Sermon," 469.

[24]Zengar, *God of Vengeance,* 85.

[25]John Mark Hicks, "The Parable of the Persistent Widow," *Restoration Quarterly* 33, no.4 (1991): 209–23.

[26]John Mark Hicks, "How to Preach a Curse," Lipscomb University Preaching Seminar, May 5–7, 1997, obtained from http://johnmarkhicks.faithsite.com/content.asp?CID=3913; and "Preaching Imprecatory Psalms," in *A Heart to Study and Teach: Essays Honoring Clyde M. Woods,* ed. Dale W. Manor (Henderson, Tenn.: Freed-Hardeman University Press, 2000), obtained from http://johnmarkhicks.faithsite.com/content.asp?CID=11789 on December 31, 2004.

[27]John Mark Hicks, *Yet Will I Trust Him* (Joplin, Mo.: College Press, 1999), 15–19.

[28]Walter Brueggemann, *The Message of the Psalms: A Theological Commentary* (Minneapolis: Augsburg, 1984), 68.

[29]Ibid., 67.

[30]Daniel L. Migliore and Kathleen D. Billman, *Rachel's Cry: Prayer of Lament and Rebirth of Hope* (Cleveland: United Church Press, 1999).

[31]W. E. B. Du Bois, *The Souls of Black Folk,* 186, obtained from http://etext.lib.virginia.edu/toc/modeng/public/DubSoul.html on December 31, 2004.

[32]See the 9/11 lament by Rabbi Peter H. Schweitzer, obtained from http://www.humanistjew.org/Lamentation.htm on December 31, 2004.

[33]For worship resources, see J. Frank Henderson, *Liturgies of Lament* (Chicago: Liturgy Training Publications, 1994). Cf. Michael Borgert, "Bibliography of Biblical and Pastoral Resources on Lament," *Calvin Theological Journal* 38, no. 2 (2003): 335–40.

Chapter 5: The New Testament Preaches the Psalms

[1]A study of the psalms and the history of their interpretation is also a study in the theological and social history of Christianity and Judaism. The oft-cited counter example is, of course, the Antiochene school of exegesis from the patristic period. The Antiochenes appear to have been more sensitive to the historical context of the psalmists than their exegetical nemeses, the Alexandrians. In truth, the issues are more complex, and the motivation for the Antiochenes was not as objective as we (perhaps) think ours are. See Frances Young, *Biblical Exegesis and the Formation of Christian Culture* (Cambridge: Cambridge University Press, 1997).

[2]See W. L. Holladay, *The Psalms through Three Thousand Years: Prayerbook of a Cloud of Witnesses* (Minneapolis: Fortress Press, 1993), 129: "But because the New Testament became canonical for Christians, its mode of using the Psalms (and other Old Testament material) became canonical. This circumstance immediately raises for Christians the question of how one deals theologically with any disparity between a given text in the Old Testament and a use of the same text in the New Testament."

[3]"Pesher," Hebrew for "interpretation," is a "cover term" scholars have given to a mode of scriptural exposition practiced at Qumran, a continuous running commentary on a biblical text.

[4]See James C. VanderKam, *The Dead Sea Scrolls Today* (Grand Rapids, Mich.: Eerdmans, 1994), 71–119.

[5]Ibid., 32.

[6]We see both aspects brought together in the Psalms Scroll (11 QPsa).

[7]We should not, however, be surprised. The Psalms have a very interesting history in the Second Temple period, especially given that so many of them originated in the First Temple liturgy. It is worthwhile to consider the process of canonization (which may not have been finished by the period of Qumran settlement or even the NT), the editing and addition of superscriptions, the theological significance placed on the Psalms by the chronicler, etc. See Holladay, *Psalms through Three Thousand Years,* 67–91.

[8]The historical superscriptions of the Psalms, which clearly come later than the Psalms themselves, historicize the Psalms in the sense of tying them back to the life and times of David.

[9]11QPsa *David's Composition.* Translations of the Dead Sea Scrolls come from *The Dead Sea Scrolls: Study Edition,* ed. and trans. Florentino García Martínez and Eibert J. C. Tigchelaar, 2 vols. (Leiden: Brill; and Grand Rapids, Mich.: Eerdmans, 1997).

[10]Mt. 22:43 and Mk. 12:36. Psalm 110 comes from "David by the Spirit"; Acts 1:16: Pss. 69:25 and 109:8 are the foretelling of "the Holy Spirit through David"; Acts 4:25: Ps. 2:1–2 are "said by the Holy Spirit through our ancestor David"; Heb 4:7: God speaks Ps. 95:7b "through David."

[11]Presumably, it is because of David's authorship that Jesus can group the Psalms alongside "the law of Moses" and "the prophets" as texts that are fulfilled by his death and resurrection. "These are my words that I spoke to you while I was still with you— that everything written about me in the law of Moses, the prophets, and *the psalms* must be fulfilled" (Lk. 24:44, emphasis added).

[12]For an exception, see our discussion of Ps. 95:7b-11 below.

[13]See Mt. 22:44//Mk. 12:36//Lk. 20:42–43; Mt. 26:64//Mk. 14:62; Acts 2:34; 7:55–56; Rom. 8:34; Eph. 1:20; Col. 3:1; Heb. 1:3, 13; 8:1; 10:12; 12:2; and 1 Pet. 3:22.

[14]There is one exception: Heb. 5:6 speaks to the context of Ps. 110:1 when it refers to Ps. 110:4 ("You are a priest forever according to the order of Melchizedek"). This line is also read as a prophetic reference to Christ and serves as the Hebrews author's basis for claiming Christ to be a priest. Hebrews associates Jesus' priesthood with his sitting at God's right hand in 8:1 and 10:12. This association strikes me as an innovation on the part of the author rather than an established tradition (like using Ps. 110:1 as code for referring to the ascension). Indeed, Hebrews mutes any sense of Christ as the enthroned king in Ps. 110:1 by emphasizing him as priest from v. 4.

[15]"Pesherim" is the plural of pesher, Hebrew for "interpretation" (see n. 3). There is a nearly complete set of pesherim for Ps. 37 in 4Q 171 (4QPsalms Peshera). See *The Dead Sea Scrolls Study Edition,* 343–47.

[16]VanderKam (*Dead Sea Scrolls Today,* 44) notes "two fundamental assumptions underlay Qumran exegesis. The first is that the *biblical writer* referred in his prophecy to the latter days, not to his own time; the second was that the *commentator* assumed he was living during the latter days and that therefore the ancient prophecies were directed to his own days. His duty, then, was to unlock the secrets of the prophets' mysterious words and thus to find the divine message that addressed his circumstances."

[17]4Q171 (or 4 *QpPsa*) IV.26–27: "And my tongue is the pen of [a skilled scribe. Its interpretation] concerns the Teach[er of Righteousness...befo]re God with the reply of the tongue."

[18]The Hebrews author is quoting the Septuagint translation (LXX) here. The differences between the LXX and the Hebrew texts of Ps. 95:7b-11 are modest and do not have any major impact on our discussion.

[19]The enthronement psalms consist of Pss. 93–99, though Ps. 94's status as such is disputed. J. Clinton McCann, "Psalms," in *New Interpreter's Bible,* ed. Leander Keck et al., vol. 4 (Nashville: Abingdon Press, 1996), 662. See also James Mays, *The Lord Reigns: A Theological Handbook to the Psalms* (Louisville: Westminster John Knox Press, 1994), 12–22.

[20]McCann, "Psalms," 1062.

[21]The Hebrew word for "listen" is *shema,* which also connotes obedience.

[22]Other possible oracles in the Psalms are Pss. 12:5; 32:8–9; 50:7–15, 16–23; 81:8–13. See Roland E. Murphy, *The Gift of the Psalms* (Peabody, Mass.: Hendrickson, 2000), 120.

[23]I consider the author's frankness and harsh words to be a stylistic feature he has appropriated from contemporary moral philosophy (see Philodemus, *On Frank Speech,* and Plutarch, *How to Tell A Flatterer From A Friend).*

[24]Harold Attridge, *The Epistle to the Hebrews,* Hermeneia (Philadelphia: Fortress Press, 1989), 123–24.

[25]On the historical perspective in Qumran and NT exegesis, see part 1 above.

[26]The rabbis called exegesis by means of linking a term in one passage with a term in another *gezera shawa.* The link only works with the LXX translations of the two passages and not in the Hebrew text.

[27]See the very detailed and helpful discussion in Attridge, *Hebrews,* 129–30.

[28]LXX Psalm 94:1 "Song of Praise to David" is lacking in the Hebrew text of Psalm 95.

[29]See also the interpretation of Jer. 31:31–34 in Hebrews 8 and again in 10:32.

[30]"Exhort one another every day, as long as it is called 'today,' so that none of you may be hardened by the deceitfulness of sin" (Heb. 3:13).

[31]Cf. Acts 2:23, where Peter says Jesus is handed over to the Jewish leaders "according to the definite plan and foreknowledge of God."

[32]Note the awkward plural in Acts 4:27, "the *peoples* of Israel." This plural preserves the link with Ps. 2:1 ("the *peoples* plot in vain").

[33]Speaking the word boldly is a pivotal point in this chapter, as can be seen in the threefold repetition of *parressia,* "boldness" (4:13, 29, 31; cf. 28:31).

[34]In my discussion of Psalm 2, I follow the exposition in Patrick D. Miller, *Interpreting the Psalms* (Philadelphia: Fortress Press, 1986), 87–93.

[35]On the difficulty of the Hebrew text, see McCann, "Psalms," 690.

[36]Luke Timothy Johnson argues that Acts 4:23–31 is specifically the prayer of the apostles and not the believers in general. See his *The Acts of the Apostles,* Sacra Pagina 5 (Collegeville, Minn: Liturgical Press, 1992), 83.

[37]Miller, *Interpreting the Psalms,* 88–89.

[38]On the collusion between the Roman governors and the leaders of Israel, see especially Acts 24–25, where Luke states a number of times that Paul is kept in prison by Roman governors Felix and Festus "as a favor" to the Jews.

[39]Cf. Walter Brueggemann ("The Psalms as Limit Expressions," chapter 2 in this volume) when he discusses how Psalms similar to Ps. 22 function so as "to give permission and authority to the congregation to practice candor in its own life in the presence of God."

[40]Holladay, *The Psalms through Three Thousand Years,* 119: "the lament psalms [especially those of the righteous sufferer] were a primary tool in the early church for theological interpretation of the passion narrative."

[41]Raymond Brown, *Death of the Messiah: From Gethsemane to the Grave: A Commentary on the Passion Narratives in the Four Gospels* (New York: Doubleday, 1994), 1049.

[42]Matthew strengthens the association between Ps. 22 and the passion narrative he inherited from Mark.

[43] *The Revised Psalms of the New American Bible* (New York: Catholic Book, 1991), 41; cf. James L. Mays, *Psalms,* Interpretation (Louisville: Westminster John Knox Press, 1994), 106.

[44]The numbering of verses in Psalm 22 in the *New American Bible* translation begins with the inscription. Thus verses 2–12 in NAB are verses 1–11 in NRSV. NAB verses discussed in this section all follow that pattern.

[45]The psalmist describes his enemies as "bulls" (Ps. 22:13, 22, NAB), "lions" (vv. 14, 22, NAB), and "dogs" (vv. 17, 21, NAB).

[46]Mays, *Psalms,* 112–13.

[47]Given the resurrection pericope (Mk. 16) to follow, the concluding praise section of Ps. 22 ought not be wholly discarded.

[48]John R. Donahue, S.J., and Daniel J. Harrington, S.J., *The Gospel of Mark,* Sacra Pagina 2 (Collegeville, Minn.: Liturgical Press, 2002), 445.

[49]Ibid., 445.

[50]Mays, *Psalms,* 105.

[51]Ibid., 113.

[52]A. Katherine Grieb, "Vindication: The Cross as Good News for Women," *Christian Century* 116 (1999): 1020–21.

Chapter 6: Reading the Psalms for Preaching

[1]Gerald T. Sheppard, "Theology and the Book of Psalms," *Interpretation* 46 (April, 1992): 145.

[2]Augustine, *On Christian Doctrine,* trans. D. W. Robinson Jr. (Indianapolis: Bobbs-Merrill, 1958).

[3]Ibid., 9.

[4]Ibid., 11, 12.

[5]Ibid., 8.

[6]See Paul Scott Wilson, *God Sense: Reading the Bible for Preaching* (Nashville: Abingdon Press, 2001), esp. 57–68.

[7]Augustine, "Discourse on Psalm 3," in *St. Augustine on the Psalms,* trans. Dame Scholastica Hebgin & Dame Felicitas Corrigan, Ancient Christian Writers, vol. 1 (Westminster, Md.: Newman Press, 1960), 30.

[8]Ibid., 30.

[9]Ibid., 30–31.

[10]Ibid., 31–32.

[11]Ibid., 32.

[12]Cited by James Anderson, "Introductory Notice," in John Calvin, *Commentary on the Book of Psalms,* trans. James Anderson, vol. 1 (Grand Rapids, Mich.: Eerdmans, 1949), vii.

[13]T. H. L. Parker, *Calvin's Preaching* (Louisville: Westminster John Knox Press, 1992), 63.

[14]John H. Leith, "John Calvin," in *Concise Encyclopedia of Preaching,* ed. William H. Willimon and Richard Lischer (Louisville: Westminster John Knox Press, 1995), 62.

[15]Calvin, *Commentary,* 27.

[16]Ibid., 28.

[17]Ibid., 32.

[18]Ibid., 33.

[19]J. Clinton McCann, Jr., "The Book of Psalms: Introduction, Commentary and Reflections," in *The New Interpreter's Bible: A Commentary in Twelve Volumes,* vol. 4 (Nashville: Abingdon Press, 1996), 639–1280.

[20]Ibid., 646.

[21]Ibid., 694.

²²Ibid.

²³Ibid., 693.

²⁴Clinton McCann, Jr., and James C. Howell, *Preaching the Psalms* (Nashville: Abingdon Press, 2001), 51.

²⁵McCann, "Book of Psalms," 695.

²⁶Ibid., 665.

²⁷James Luther Mays, *Psalms: A Bible Commentary for Teaching and Preaching* (Louisville: Westminster John Knox Press, 1994), 23.

²⁸Hans Frei, *The Eclipse of Biblical Narrative* (New Haven, Conn.: Yale University Press, 1974).

²⁹Ibid., 10.

³⁰Julian N. Hartt, *Theological Method and Imagination* (New York: Seabury Press, 1977), 237.

³¹Reading the Psalms with imagination is one of seven principles that Carroll Stuhlmueller says is essential for understanding them. Carroll Stuhlmueller, O.P., *The Spirituality of the Psalms* (Collegeville, Minn.: Liturgical Press, 2002), 13–15.

³²Frei, *Eclipse,* 14–15.

³³Ibid., 15.

³⁴Mays, *Psalms,* 53.

³⁵I have spoken about this at length in Paul Scott Wilson, *The Four Pages of the Sermon: A Guide to Biblical Preaching* (Nashville: Abingdon Press, 1999), 28–29, 90–106, 130–54, 174–98, 213–34.

³⁶See McCann and Howell for a brief discussion of *Sitz im Leben* and Psalms 70–72.

³⁷For example, McCann notes that some scholars divide the Psalm into three units: "vv. 1–3 (the foes and God's response), vv. 4–6 (the psalmist and God), vv. 7–8 (petition and profession)," 694. Variations in division presumably prompt variation in fictive plot.

³⁸The most thorough treatment of how one might preach from the Old Testament and speak of Christ is Sidney Greidanus, *Preaching Christ from the Old Testament: A Contemporary Hermeneutical Method* (Grand Rapids, Mich. and Cambridge, U.K.: Eerdmans, 1999). For a helpful essay on how Jesus used the Psalms, see J. Clinton McCann, Jr., "The Psalms and Jesus Christ," in *A Theological Introduction to the Book of Psalms: The Psalms as Torah* (Nashville: Abingdon Press, 1993), 163–75.

³⁹Mays, *Psalms,* 30.

⁴⁰Wilson, *God Sense.*

⁴¹McCann and Howell, in addition to their suggestion for preachers to focus on an image in a psalm, suggest an alternative: "So a second approach to preaching a Psalm may be to capture its inner dynamic, the energy that transports the reader to a new place" (*Preaching the Psalms,* 69). This movement presumably is a form of narrative plot that is informed by the historical *Sitz im Leben* (70–72), as indeed fictive plot is when such historical information is available. Mays on Psalm 3 recommends use of the superscriptions not as historical notices, but as "permission and encouragement to heuristic reflection, they lead to discoveries that lend concreteness and use to the liturgical language of the psalm" (*Psalms,* 54).

Chapter 7: Like a Child at Home

¹Mary Pipher, *The Shelter of Each Other: Rebuilding Our Families* (New York: Ballantine, 1996), 180.

²Thanks to Brian Caughlan for calling this to my attention.

³Pipher, *Shelter,* 94.

⁴Isaac Watts, "My Shepherd Will Supply My Need," 1719.

⁵The short story can be most easily located in Paula J. Carlson and Peter S. Hawkins, *Listening for God,* vol. 3 (Minneapolis: Augsburg Fortress Press, 2000), 142–55. The quote is on p. 149.

Chapter 8: Beauty

[1]David Bentley Hart, *The Beauty of the Infinite: The Aesthetics of Christian Truth* (Grand Rapids, Mich.: Eerdmans, 2003).
[2]J. Clinton McCann Jr., and James C. Howell, *Preaching the Psalms* (Nashville: Abingdon Press, 2001).
[3]Mark S. Smith, *Psalms: The Divine Journey* (New York: Paulist Press, 1987).
[4]Ken Follett, *Pillars of the Earth* (New York: Signet, 1989), 22.
[5]Amos Wilder, "Electric Chimes or Rams' Horns," in *Grace Confounding* (Philadelphia: Fortress Press, 1972), 13.
[6]David Halberstam, *Summer of '49* (New York: Avon, 1989), 163.
[7]Ibid., 158–59.
[8]Quoted and discussed by Thomas Dubay, *The Evidential Power of Beauty* (San Francisco: Ignatius, 1999), 306.
[9]Hans Urs von Balthasar, *The Glory of the Lord: A Theological Aesthetic,* vol. 1: *Seeing the Form,* trans. Erasmo Leiva-Merikakis (San Francisco: Ignatius, 1982), 88.
[10]Ibid., 124.
[11]John Navone, *Enjoying God's Beauty* (Collegeville, Minn.: Liturgical Press, 1999), xiii.
[12]Rowan Williams, *A Ray of Darkness* (Cambridge: Cowley, 1995), 25.

Chapter 9: Though Mountains Shake in the Sea

[1]At this point in the sermon, for a brief moment, one of the abuse pictures from Abu Ghraib prison in Iraq is displayed on the screen behind the podium. The picture depicts an Iraqi prisoner, hooded, standing on a box, with electrodes attached to him and wires dangling from his body.
[2]Here, a video clip is displayed depicting two scenes from the movie *The Matrix.* The clips are shown without setup and without sound. The first scene depicts a field of fetuses being harvested by machines and placed into the "power plant" that plugs them into the Matrix. Those who have seen the movie will recognize the Matrix as a place where impersonal forces pull a computer-generated world down over the eyes of humans. The second scene depicts the lines of computer code that run continuously down computer screens and represent the Matrix.
[3]At this moment a video clip appears on the screen from the movie *The Fifth Element.* The clip is played without setup and without sound. It depicts four explorers who find a sacred place from which they harness the power of the universe to destroy a killer meteor that threatens all of civilization, just in the nick of time.
[4]A video clip is shown without setup and without sound. The clip is from *The Matrix* and depicts Sipher, a betrayer, eating a succulent piece of steak while agreeing to reenter the Matrix.

Chapter 10: The Goodness of God

[1]Walter Brueggemann, "'Until'...Endlessly Enacted, Now Urgent," in *Inscribing the Text: Sermons and Prayers of Walter Brueggemann,* ed. Anna Carter Florence (Minneapolis: Fortress Press, 2004).
[2]See chapter 1, p. 26, in this volume.
[3]When McCann presented his lecture at Rochester College, he played Sweet Honey in the Rock's song "Greed," which I quote in this sermon.
[4]James Crenshaw, "Standing Near the Flame: Psalm 73," in *The Psalms: An Introduction* (Grand Rapids: Eerdmans, 2001), 114.
[5]Russell Conwell, *Acres of Diamonds* (Westwood, N.J.: Fleming H. Revell, 1960), 24.
[6]Richard Hughes, *Myths America Lives By* (Urbana: University of Illinois Press, 2003), 149.